Rayna Noire Books

Fiction

Initiation

Revelation

Declaration

Affirmation

Pagan Eyes Collection

Glimmer

Smolder

Blaze

Birdbrain (October 2019)

Non-fiction

Communicating with Your Animal Messengers

In Harmony

In Harmony

Learn to Live in Harmony with Your Natural, Physical and Spiritual Worlds

Rayna Noire

Table of Contents

Preface

MOST OF US WILL ACKNOWLEDGE that we have a mental, physical, and spiritual sphere. If we decide to lose weight, that occurs in the physical world, where we control what we eat and jog around the running track. We might enter the mental world when we try to outthink the criminal in a crime drama. The spiritual world is often confined to a few hours per week, usually inside a church.

The different spheres exist and consistently interact—rather like a VENN diagram that consists of two interlocking circles. The area between the circles is what is shared. I came to this realization when I went to the dentist. My mother had died, and there was some family drama about how my stepfather had treated the whole situation. The dental hygienist asked me if something traumatic had happened recently. That made me wonder why she'd ask such a question. Was she psychic? No. She explained the teeth and gums reflect what is going on in our lives. My emotional and mental wellbeing bled over into my physical self.

When I go to yoga—a series of physical moves accompanied by rhythmic breathing—I always finish the class mentally cleansed and, sometimes, spiritually uplifted. Sometimes, it is easy to see how the spheres connect. Other times, not so much.

When we work on one sphere, we improve another.

When you take a walk in the woods, it's a physical endeavor. The greenness of nature and the sound of running water calms your mental state and can even open you up to spiritual insights.

When I tried to exercise, my mental state improved. When I meditate, which is part of the spiritual sphere, both my mental and physical health improved. This book is about all three spheres and is divided into Mental, Spiritual, and Physical. However, each essay could easily fit into more than one sphere.

Feel free to accept the messages that serve you and reject those that don't. My end goal is to share insights I have learned over the years that have enriched and unified my spheres of existence.

Pearls on a String

BUDDHA LEFT HIS PALACE AND his wife when he met a beggar at the palace gates. He was unaware of those who weren't royal before then. For six years, he wandered his country, often working and eating with those he met. Most were poor, some were not, but he concluded they were all essential. When he returned to the palace, he shared his adventures.

The teachers, his family, and palace workers all sat with him as he explained they were all pearls on a string. Each pearl touches another one. None of us exist alone. Even though the centerpiece pearl may not be able to see the smaller pearls at the clasp, it doesn't mean they don't exist.

Everyone on this planet is interconnected. Technology has allowed us to connect and, at the same time, isolate ourselves. People often live their lives by interacting as little as possible with others. They drive into their garages or parking spaces never greeting or even seeing their neighbors. After work, people return home where they entertain themselves by using a variety of screens.

With such a strong emphasis on individuality and having it your way, many people are ignored as not being the right type of person. Many important learning experiences never happen. Many of us missed out on a great friend or even mate. We spend most of all leisure time in safe environments that don't allow us to grow. Our souls don't develop as they should.

Mark Twain is known for having said, "Do the thing you fear most, and the death of fear is certain". I'm sure he wasn't talking about running in front of a fast-moving train. Even changing routine is challenging for many.

Start with a little change. Don't assume you know the story behind the man who always begs at the intersection. Be open to making new friends. Even when people do things that irritate you, look for the big picture.

I've worked with special needs children my entire educational career. Many of my students don't react well to fire alarms, but the state requires that we have them. One of my students who towered over me, did respond violently to the shrill alarm. As I was herding the kids out the door, I yelled for headphones, which the speech teacher gave me. The child stopped swinging at the other students once the headphones were on. After the fire alarm, I returned the headphones, but the speech teacher was very cool and distant to me. This went on for two weeks until I asked her what was wrong. I was told by shouting for the headphones, I'd implied that she wasn't as important as the other staff.

No, I hadn't said that at all. She managed to ignore the alarm and the acting out child, focusing on what mattered to her. She did not feel as if she were a pearl on the necklace.

Sometimes, it's not enough for you to know we are all interconnected, you must share that knowledge, too.

Different Paths

IN A CLASS ON DEATH and dying, one of the students questioned the teacher about people who don't act as if they're aware of their soul's journey. Basically, the questioner felt the subject of her inquiry didn't share her personal beliefs, which she thought were the right ones.

The other students listened intently, wondering what would be the soft-spoken teacher's response. She nodded at the questioner, managed a slight smile, and cushioned her words with a warning not to take her remark too personally. She then added it wasn't her business, nor was it the student's concern by explaining to all of us.

"Each of us has a journey and a purpose, which is our business. How others react is not our business. We have no clue what their soul's purpose is. Even though it might not appear that way to us, they could be fulfilling their soul's purpose."

I remember those words whenever I have difficulty when others don't believe the way I do. My desire is to convert them to my way of thinking just like the earnest missionaries who knock on my door on the weekends, often interrupting meals or leisure activities. I'm not interested in their spiel, but I treat them politely, and wish them well as I close the door.

Many probably have treated me the same way in my desire to bring them to the *true* way. When I was a member of a mainline church, our youth minister made us go to the mall and witness to people against their wills and usually against ours, too. I hated that experience; aware I was annoying and interrupting what may have been an enjoyable day or scarce leisure time. Odd how I forgot that.

As a teenager, I tried out several schools of thought that were different from how I was raised. When I went to college, I used to sit with friends of different faiths, often talking into the night about life, beliefs, and the future. Sometimes, there would be arguments that ended amicably, since we treasured our friendship over any belief system.

One of the students, who was studying to be a minister, admitted to having an epiphany about organized religion. He felt all religions were part of a huge glass bowl that held many truths and united all, but somewhere in time, the bowl splintered. Each group picked up a shard of the vessel, calling it their religion. It could be the reason many religions are similar. Over time, many of the various followers decided their religion was the only true one. Then came some manner of judgment, often at varying times in history.

Rulers of kingdoms, and often religions, decided to sanitize their worlds by getting rid of competing religions. Sometimes, an edict went out. Other times, those with different beliefs were banished. Eventually, those with different faiths were labeled as evil and killed—even pregnant women and children. The incredible fear that drove one religion to wipe out another was, and is, often fanned by those with a thirst for power. Scary scenarios are painted to create fear.

As a veteran, I went through boot camp, often questioning the use of the term, *Charlie*. We were told *Charlie* was out to get us and everyone we cared about. Over and over, we were told to watch out for *Charlie*, the enemy. Our instructors described *Charlie* as being

Asian, but it could refer to any enemy. While I was in the army, we were not at war, and there was no real enemy. Soldiers have been trained by creating a phantom enemy for centuries. Politics works the same. As do many religions.

When I react, trying to convince someone of their wrong-minded ideas by telling them mine, I am on the same type of mission, without a gun or sword, to drive home my point. In Erich Maria Remarque's book, *All Quiet on the Western Front*, the main character, a young German soldier, finds himself wrestling with an injured French soldier. The Frenchman asks the young soldier to write a letter to his wife and children so they will know how he died. At that moment, he sees the dying soldier as a man like him, as opposed to the enemy.

When we meet people of differing beliefs, we often make judgments—not necessarily accurate—limited by our own beliefs and perceived knowledge. If we could soar high above the situation like a hawk, then we could see the big picture. We'd see that while we all have our own path and our own soul journey, eventually, all paths combine to make a whole. The splintered bowl would eventually become whole again, and all that did not make sense before would be perfectly clear.

As for now, our job is to unconditionally love our fellow travelers and to remember their business is not ours.

Meditation

ALMOST ANY RECENT MEDICAL BOOK will tell you the value of meditation, but they fail to explain how and why. Most of us imagine a monk sitting in a full lotus position, stilling his mind for hours on end. Dinty W. Moore in his book, *The Accidental Buddhist,* spent many hours struggling with the concept of meditation. He considered himself a failure because other thoughts kept entering his head when he should have been void of thought. One day, he could ask a teacher about this very issue.

The teacher nodded his head and replied that it was normal, and even the more senior monks had issues with outside thoughts intruding. Instead of getting upset, the teacher explained to accept the intruding thought, then send it on its way. It was a freeing moment for the anxious student, who couldn't understand why he never was able to achieve a perfect, thoughtless state.

Sometimes, rather than thinking of achieving a thoughtless state, think of it as touching the universe. We do this all the time when we are in the zone. This could be anything from running, being in nature, dancing, working with crystals, or yoga. Even the act of coloring can be a form of meditation. Anything we totally give ourselves over to can be meditative. You know when you're in the zone because time has slipped away. Often, you have no desire to eat or drink because you're so focused.

Intention precedes meditation. You create the intention to

meditate. This will involve setting aside a time and place. It's as simple as taking five deep breaths and concentrating on your breathing. It doesn't have to be too long. The meditative practice has an energy of its own. Each time you meditate, the energy remains. This is why many people use meditative stones, mats, or the same place in which to meditate. The energy remains and builds, making it easier to meditate each time. Others wear a crystal that absorbs the energy.

Still others find it hard to shut out the outside world. Not too strange considering we are constantly accustomed to having screen time and being blasted with the thoughts and words of others. It will take effort to quiet your mind. Some use environmental sounds or even guided meditations to help, of which many are available on YouTube.

Meditation has many benefits, both medical and spiritual. It helps people heal faster, calms, and centers. By using the loving-kindness meditation, I was able to let go of lingering resentment.

There are all kinds of meditation, from walking through a forest to gazing at a candle flame. Everyone is capable of something. By meditating, we draw closer to our true center.

The Gathering of Things

THERE IS AN ONLINE PEER to peer counseling site called Quora where people post questions and other people answer. Most of the answers are thoughtful. A few are flippant and not helpful. It is up to the poster to decide if any information will work.

The other day someone asked why do obviously evil people have so much and are so blessed by material wealth? This is a question people have wrestled with for centuries. I remember such a question coming from the pulpit when I was a young girl. The minister's answer was that the person may have a lot of stuff now, but the Christian God would take it away eventually. It seemed to please the congregation that someone they thought of as an unbeliever would lose all they worked for.

This same sentiment could have been expressed in a nearby temple, synagogue, mosque, or small group meeting. What the minister should have said was that material things don't matter in the end. You can't take them with you, even though ancient people were often buried with some of the favorite trinkets and weapons. Often, those who did have money and stuff, leave behind warring relatives who turn on each other to make sure they get their share.

Even my grandmother, who led a modest life and never owned a car, left behind a roomful of items. There were some arguments about who should have what. These arguments didn't honor the loving woman she was. In retrospect, I can understand how people thought they were somehow holding on to a part of her. They weren't. After all, it was only stuff. Because my grandmother hadn't been rich, the items were of poor quality and out of date. I wonder how many people still have the items they felt were worth fighting for.

Due to reality television, we now know there are hoarders everywhere. When asked why, the hoarders explain that the surplus of out of date newspapers and stack of Styrofoam trays bring them comfort and security. When, the items cause the person to be isolated and often create a health risk. Somehow, we have decided in Western Culture that having more is somehow winning the game of Life.

My grandmother turned deaf at an early age and eventually died from ALS, which is a horrible way to go. Yet, she was always grateful for all she had and extremely generous. As a child, I used to ask her what was the best blessing. She always told me good health no matter how many times I asked. It was never a sports car or a fancy mansion. As a kid who had robust health, I took it for granted, and couldn't understand why a person would want a health blessing.

There wasn't as much stuff decades ago as there is now, but I did know we were poor and most other people had more than us, from nice clothes to meat at every meal. Just walking through my modest neighborhood, I saw driveways crammed with vehicles for each member of the family with no room in the garage for their vehicles which served instead as an overflow area for all their excess. Years ago, we managed with one car or no car.

It is no wonder the Quora questioner wondered why some of the people have all the stuff. It isn't necessarily a blessing. Those who have plenty often don't appreciate what they have. They often suspect others of stealing or using their property. The very wealthy can become as isolated as the person collecting Styrofoam meat trays.

Things don't make you happy. While I've never had a chance to be wealthy, I have rubbed elbows with a few people with multiple homes and personal jets. They had moments of joy, but most of their life was spent guarding their possessions rather like dragons. The rest of the time they labored to make more money that they spent on more stuff. It is rather ironic. They had to come to a non-wealthy person, me, to experience fun.

In the movie, *Happy*, the narrator finds some of the happiest people are those in the poorest countries. They measure their happiness not by things, but by the welcoming smile of their child or having a meal of rice and vegetables to share. In the movie, Americans did not fare well. They spent too much time comparing themselves to others who had more stuff.

According to the Gallup poll, the average world household income is about nine thousand per household, which includes *all* the adults in the household working. It reminds me of the story of a man who went to teach in the Philippines several years ago. When he arrived, a young boy approached him and asked to be his house boy. The teacher explained he wasn't rich and couldn't afford a servant. The boy then asked if the teacher had a place to live and more than one pair of shoes. The teacher agreed he did, which made him rich to the boy who had no home or shoes. The youngster only wanted someplace to sleep at night and something to eat. The teacher allowed the boy to live with him.

Perception

GROWING UP I HAD A perception disability along with extreme buck teeth. I was often teased and ridiculed by other students, even adults. To some extent, I knew the laughter was directed at me, but I couldn't always see it was meant to humiliate me. Often, I accepted sarcasm as literal. If someone told me I had a beautiful smile when they meant to ridicule my teeth, I would thank them. I'm sure I frustrated my tormenters.

In some ways, my disability protected me. I didn't realize, until I went into special needs training, that I even had this issue. One of the students in my classroom had a similar disability and kids would tease him. It didn't upset him as it would most kids. It only confused him since he took everything literally. His father pulled him out of the public school and enrolled him in a special school. I often wondered if the father was doing his son any favors. We all have perceptional issues. Most aren't labeled as disabilities, though.

A revenge movie parading as a Christmas movie had a group of jilted girlfriends conspiring to make the ex-boyfriend suffer. They decided to ruin his company Christmas party by inviting random strangers to it. The ditzy ex-girlfriend invites several people from a biker bar. The lawyer ex is against this, thinking she went too far. Her perception was the biker people were somehow farther down the pecking order than anyone else.

We all do this to some extent. That's the purpose behind labels.

There are a ton of them—heathen, Pagan, infidel, sloppy, lazy, stupid, etc. When I visited India, I was impressed by how careful everyone was about their appearance. On our first day there, we walked to a nearby shopping mall. With our height and complexion announcing us as foreigners, we had been briefed by hotel personnel not to give anyone money. On our way, a lady in an ironed sari and combed hair tried to get our attention with her baby. The other shoppers made a wide circle around the woman and child.

Eventually, she came close enough to us to pat our arms. Her child did likewise. When we drew near our hotel with its armed guards and a security fence the woman fell back. We learned that she was considered untouchable. People actually paid not to be touched by her or her family members by a caste system created long ago that still imprisons the people. One of the hotel employees told me with pride, how, having been born into a higher caste, he could own his own restaurant within the hotel. It made no sense to me that this woman, who took such care with her appearance, should be feared if she might encounter someone. It reminded me of the childhood game, Cooties, where the one with cooties tries to touch others who always ran away.

On the way home, we tried to understand. This caste system is basically based on the color of skin and jobs from long ago. For a moment, I may have felt superior, thinking our country did not have such a system, but we do. We place those with money, beauty, youth, and fame at the top.

Patricia Moore, a social scientist, wanted to test her theory that the old were treated differently and disguised herself as three different elderly ladies. One was a bag lady, another a middle-class patron, and the third, a wealthy matriarch. As the poor woman, she was often ignored and assaulted. She was beaten so badly by a gang of twelve-year-old boys that it had lasting effects. The middle-class woman was often ignored, sometimes cheated, but eventually grudgingly waited upon. Only the wealthy matriarch was treated well, and only because those who helped her expected a tip.

A friend of mine shared how people cross the street when they see her oldest son. All they see is a big, black dude with a beard and wrongly assume trouble. They don't see his bookishness, his shyness, or his love for his family. Perceptions can work in the opposite way, too.

One of my students was a very handsome young man. He often stopped people in their tracks because everything about him was physically perfect from his hair to his body. Because I worked with him, I noticed immediately that he cheated and lied. He often tricked other students, too. Still, other students would give him unlimited chances, especially the girls. The football coach and other teachers gave him leeway he didn't deserve. They couldn't believe he was undeserving.

As a person who witnessed his many acts of cruelty, I was shocked that people constantly rewarded him while ignoring less attractive students who were much more deserving. Who knows? Maybe it had something to do with my perceptional disability that I didn't see him as others did.

In retrospect, I think perception is another world for prejudice. We need to keep checking our perceptions. Otherwise, we could be missing out on people we need to know. We could also be missing out on experiences that could enrich our lives.

Accountability and Forgiveness

MOST RELIGIONS TEACH FORGIVENESS. PEOPLE naturally assume the forgiveness is for the person who committed the transgression. Often the person who caused the problem believes forgiveness wipes out the action and consequences from it. For example, in many of the twelve-step programs, they encourage the offender to go back to those they have abused and ask for forgiveness. The offender could have torn families apart, stolen, beaten, or even raped the survivor. Not too surprisingly, this person does not want to see the offender.

My husband dealt with a drug-addicted ex who ripped his life apart and robbed him before moving on. He was left with nothing except the bills she'd run up. At one point, she called and wanted to come by and ask for his forgiveness as part of her program. He refused. He didn't want to mend their relationship. Instead, he wanted accountability. He wanted her to financially repay him for all the bills he'd paid and for everything she stole. Unfortunately, she didn't want accountability—*just a pat on the hand and to be told to forget about it.*

Forgiveness is sometimes used as a get out of jail free card. An acquaintance felt sorry for himself, drank too much, then drove down a street crowded with parked cars. He bounced off dozens of cars causing thousands of dollars' worth of damage. He wasn't caught initially and felt as if asking for forgiveness in front of the church should be enough. After all, he felt bad about what he did.

He later discovered one of the destroyed cars belonged to a church member who needed his car for work. Forgiveness wasn't enough. The member needed a working car to get to his job. He did eventually confess, received probation and had to pay damages. Would it have been different if no church members had their cars banged up?

Everything has repercussions even if we don't immediately see the result. There are plenty of anecdotes about a bully who teased the class nerd only to discover later the nerd owns the company where the bully wanted a job.

Instead of forgiveness, why not emphasize accountability? If you could not expect forgiveness, would you act differently? Ever wonder why child sexual abuse is rampant in religious institutes? My belief is that offenders rely on their ability to ask for forgiveness. There is always the death bed confession or last rites that assures your reservation in Heaven—or does it?

Agnostics and atheists can be much kinder to family members because they don't always expect automatic forgiveness. On the other hand, those who expect a divine pardon whenever they ask for it are often hateful to those they love. They are often put out when the offended person doesn't forgive them because they think of it as their right. Divine forgiveness doesn't mean you didn't do the reprehensible thing. Only that you won't be held accountable if that is your religious belief.

Every one of us is accountable for our actions. This is not just how we treat other people, but how we treat animals, resources, even nature, especially nature. Consider this. After decades of polluting, saying sorry isn't going to do anything for the current pollution problem.

My grandmother was fond of saying actions speak more loudly

than words. If a person felt responsible for the solid waste problem, then he or she could recycle, use canvas bags, avoid single-use plastics and reuse items as opposed to trashing them. That would be demonstrating accountability.

Is forgiveness ever useful? It is best used when we are stuck in a rut of beating ourselves up over something we've done in the past. We can acknowledge it happened. Decide what we learned, forgive ourselves, and let it go.

That could work with other people, too. Trust your instincts. Forgiveness is not letting toxic people back in your life. That's stupidity. My ex-husband, who tried to choke the life out of me, kept trying to reinsert himself in my life. I wouldn't let it happen. Often, we can love some people at a distance. As the decades have passed, I have learned from that situation. I have let it go and have even felt compassion for my ex, though it took decades as opposed to overnight.

Purpose

EVERYONE WANTS TO HAVE A life of purpose. Each president worries about his legacy and how media will interpret it. It's so easy to lose our self-esteem comparing ourselves to other people and what we see as their purpose. What is our purpose? Develop a cure for cancer? Wipe out hatred? Write a New York Times Best Seller?

Even though it's hard to admit, most of us will never be celebrities. The paparazzi will not follow us around or trample our daffodils for the perfect shot of us doing yard work. Most of us live ordinary lives with family and jobs.

Too often people are in competition with each other. Social media fuels this constant belief that we aren't good enough as ourselves. Not too surprising when people insist on putting up staged photos that have been enhanced to the nth degree. Sometimes, when exposed to constant television, movies, and magazines, it's hard to remember what people look like.

Disappointment lurks around every corner because you can't be anyone other than who you are. You are the best at being you. Years ago, I did a little running and discovered almost everyone was consumed with beating their personal best time. It's okay to compete with yourself.

Journaling helps to remember where you once were and what has changed in your life. Once goals have been achieved, we tend to forget how much positive progress we've made and fall into the pit of thinking we've done nothing. Sometimes, journaling helps us to remember when we did overcome obstacles.

How do we know what our purpose is? First, consider who you are. Sometimes, we ignore what we really want to do, telling ourselves it's selfish as we juggle the demands of our daily lives. Back when we were young, we'd volunteer for what we wanted to do to anyone who asked and often to a few who didn't. What happened to those dreams and desires? Better yet, how do we get them back? It could be as major as a career change, which could start by taking a class or researching the field. It could also be as simple as going to work a new way or trying one thing different a day. You could be living your ideal life, but your perception is a bit skewed.

All of us have a shared interest in improving our world every day. It can be as simple as a smile, helping someone, or even picking up trash. My daughter decided to do an act of kindness for a different elderly person every day. It changed the way she looked at older people and herself. It's safe to say we are all responsible for making the world a brighter and kinder place.

Volunteering can teach us about ourselves while helping others. Every day we are involved in creating purpose in our lives. Instead of looking at your life as ordinary or mundane, see everything as your purpose. Even though the phrase has been overused as of late, live in the moment. Do everything with great meaning. To lighten my weight, I chose to be fully aware when I ate, experiencing the food as opposed to shoveling it in as I normally did before in front of the television.

Purpose covers every aspect of your life. I have a rescue dog who needs to be walked several times a day. Sometimes, I resent the time it takes to walk him. Part of my plan was to rescue him, care for him, and appreciate the things he is teaching me as opposed to wishing my life away. When I am in the now, I can be more patient on our walks even when he wants to roll on every freshly mown law with a look of rapturous joy. These walks allow me to see a flock of geese taking off, an extraordinary experience as opposed to ordinary.

A life of purpose is one of love for everything from sunshine to homemade salsa. It allows you to see the good in one another and spurs on the desire to lift each other. Being a friend, a co-worker, a neighbor, a relative, a gardener, a pet companion, a reader, a parent, or a listener is part of a purpose-filled life. Everything we do can be meaningful, depending on how we do it.

What if you wake up tomorrow and decide everything you do has meaning? It does. Little, trivial things matter. It adds up. It's okay if you never get your image on a stamp. I imagine the people who did never wanted it anyhow. What matters is you understand everything you do as a profound impact on your world. You are responsible for the creation of your world in word and deed.

My grandmother always saw the best in everyone and not too surprisingly, everyone loved her in turn. She taught all her grandchildren they mattered. In her own way, she also instructed us in the power of self-fulfilling prophecy. With that in mind, go out and be the best version of you. It might take some reflection to decide who that is, but once you do, your life will be so much richer.

The Time is Now

EVERY JANUARY 1ST, OR EVEN a little before that, people resolve to make positive changes in their lives, anything from getting organized to exercising more. Gyms across the country are crowded with new members, causing the old members to grumble about no available treadmills. Change can be a scary thing but is ultimately beneficial. Unfortunately, it is hard to see the positive effects immediately.

Most of us must expect to live forever. We keep on planning to do things in the future. My mother was fond of telling me what she was going to do when she won the lottery. All her goals weren't incredibly lofty. She wanted to travel, which she could have done while she was alive. It might not have been traveling aboard the Queen Mary, but she could have traveled to the National Parks.

Many potential parents wait for that perfect sweet spot where both partners are established in their careers, college debt is paid off, and they live in the picture-perfect home. Somewhere down the line, they look at each other and decide they are too old to have children.

The future appears to be this perfect time when we will have more money and plenty of leisure time. An adventurous friend shared the belief she'd be visiting Russia as soon as her husband retired. Before retiring her husband became very ill, which stopped all travel. They could have travel earlier, but she betted on tomorrow.

I love the water and everything associated with the water—swimming, snorkeling, boating, etc. My favorite dream vacation spot would be on the water, and yet, I hesitated. Not because of money or time, but not wanting to be seen in a swimsuit as if I somehow didn't merit the comfort of the water because I wasn't a tiny size zero. I have since gotten past that issue.

We all have reasons for not doing what we truly want to do. There are also excuses for not leaving behind ended relationships, failed businesses, or other emotional baggage we insist on dragging everywhere we go. If for no other purpose, think of the impression we are making on those around us. Do we want our children to deny themselves the right to enjoy life? They could model their parents by playing it safe and waiting for that mythical day that never comes.

I used to play the lottery, like my mother, waiting for that moment to strike it rich when I would do many nice things to help others. Newsflash. I didn't win and used the money to buy tickets I could have used in other ways. What I could do as nice things for others was give items I no longer use to charities, make small monthly gifts, and volunteer to work at the Humane Society. These are things I do now as opposed to waiting.

Eckhart Tolle, in his book, *The Power of Now*, encourages us to go beyond the limits we put on ourselves. Time can be fluid as opposed to a solid. We treat it like a block of butter we parcel out. Some folks might have clue about the day they'll die. Most don't. Why not live full out every day. Do what you want to do right now. Be the person you've always wanted to be. Take chances.

When I was younger, I sometimes caught myself wishing for a future when I wouldn't have small children to take care of or a fulltime job. As the children grew and no longer needed me, I wished they were young again. As I got older, some of the things I waited to do, I decided I was too old to do. Suddenly, I saw a cycle of waiting, then not doing the thing I'd waited to do. The time is now.

If you set the intention, it will happen. When I neared fifty, I decided I was too old to write a book but did it anyhow. I know I have written at least forty-four books in the last eight years. If I had never started because I thought I was too old, there would be no books.

Most of my traveling I did after I was fifty, journeying across the world, seeing it from a hot air balloon and a parasail. It took me a while to realize the time is now, not tomorrow, or the next day.

Your time is now. Whatever it is, set your intention. The universe wants you to succeed and will find ways of making it possible.

Enough

A FEW YEARS AGO, THERE was some uproar because author Lori Gottlieb had written a book entitled *Marry Him: The Case for Settling for Mr. Good Enough.* Her critics complained that she was telling women not to hold out for Mr. Right, that mythical man who was royalty, a pediatric surgeon, and worked at the local soup kitchen on weekends. Ms. Gottlieb pointed out that many women abandon men or even refuse to date men that don't measure up to their mythical man.

When did enough stop being enough? I am fortunate enough to live in a three-bedroom home with two small bathrooms in a working-class neighborhood. It used to be the goal of most families in the fifties. Having a house with two bathrooms was living large. I raised a family of five with one small bathroom. Our home now is referred to as a starter home. Several young families have moved into the neighborhood, then moved out in a few years when they'd outgrown their house. Surrounding our modest neighborhood is new developments, featuring homes big enough to be hotels on a postage-stamp-sized yard. I'm not sure how people afford such large homes, but there is obviously a market for them.

As Americans, we tend to expect everything to be large from our oversized pick-up truck to our servings at a popular chain restaurant. Oversized isn't necessarily good for you. Those who chose to enjoy fine dining on cruise ships were often upset at their small portions. What they didn't realize are the portions were the recommended serving for an adult. There's a point when enough is plenty. Any more is overkill.

Studies have shown that children who have more than ten toys are often bored. They are overwhelmed because they don't know what to play with and end up doing nothing. So why have we abandoned enough? It used to be the backbone of Irish blessings.

May you have enough happiness to keep you sweet,
enough trials to keep you strong,
enough sorrow to keep you human,
enough hope to keep you happy,
enough failure to keep you humble,
enough success to keep you eager,
enough friends to give you comfort,
enough faith and courage in yourself to banish sadness,
enough wealth to meet your needs and one thing more;
enough determination to make each day a more
wonderful day than the one before.

People used to be content with enough money to pay their bills or enough to eat. Instead of being grateful, many want more. Even demand more. Sometimes, they complain about not having enough when they really do. Enough used to be a good thing. Too often, people assume having more than you need is a good thing. Over a third of lottery winners end up declaring bankruptcy when they weren't bankrupt before they won.

Be grateful for everything. Every bite that goes into your mouth.

Appreciate your family and spouse during good and bad times. Enjoy the weather even if is gloomy and rainy. Be thankful for your job. Rejoice in your celebrations. Be happy with enough.

Surprisingly, when you celebrate your enough, more will come.

Love Yourself 24/7

SOME OF THE CRITICAL, MOST difficult people you meet do not love themselves. They might even fool you by trumpeting triumphs and showing off their newest toys. That isn't love or acceptance. It is merely an attempt to inspire some envy. If you're jealous of them, then they matter.

When a person is okay with who he or she is, the approval of others or envy isn't needed. Those who are okay with themselves are much easier to be around. They aren't busy trying to convert individuals to their school of thought, whatever it might be. My mother was like that. Everything she did was superior to anything I did. When we went out to dinner, if she ordered fish and I got steak, she would spend the rest of the meal telling me why her selection was superior with the implication that mine was lacking.

This was pretty much how it was about everything from clothes to church. She didn't just share this attitude with me, either. It wasn't too surprising when her grandchildren didn't want to be around her. No area was off-limits from a person's weight to a lack of a partner. Most people might think she felt superior to others. She tried in so many ways and even used religion to try to make herself feel better, often naming all the various people going to Hell while she was headed to Heaven.

As I grew older, it wasn't hard to see my mother was an unhappy person who didn't love herself or her life. Her critical comments initially made me feel inferior and not very happy with myself until I rejected them. I wanted to eat steak, wear the clothes of my choosing, and marry who I wanted. Eventually, I got to a place where I was okay with who I was. While I am far from a perfect person, this is who I need to be to accomplish my soul's purpose. Once I realized that, everything else was easy.

Most of us are going to come up short when we compare ourselves to celebrities or movie stars. Even the actual people have little in common with their public image. With heavy photoshopping of the magazine and digital images, even models don't look normal. One fashion magazine decided not to use live models because actual humans were not thin enough. To think, young girls are comparing themselves to pixels.

When I focused on what I was instead of what I wasn't, it made me happier and content with where I was. This came after not being able to walk normally for two years due to chronic foot pain. I'd only wanted to walk without pain. Gone was my desire to be a model-thin or the envy of others. I wanted to walk without limping or appearing to imitate Dr. Frankenstein's lame assistant, Igor.

Take into consideration how, according to reincarnation beliefs, you picked your body, parents, and life to reach your Karmic goals. It's hard to beat yourself up for something you decided in a more enlightened state. Those who don't believe in reincarnation tend to look at life from a victim mentality. When you want to complain or place blame for what you perceive to be bad things in your life, consider a victim always remains a victim. To move ahead and change things, you must be accountable. Examine to what part of the situation you contributed, but do it with love. With time, what was viewed as a tragedy when it was happening, such as being fired or a divorce, becomes only a lesson.

Treat yourself like a precious treasure because you are. Everyone who exists at this moment in time has a divine purpose. When you can be kind to yourself, it will be easy to be kind to others. When your self-talk consists of positive statements, instead of negative criticism, you can share that attitude with others, too.

Take time for yourself. It is never wasted. Many people are rushing around with their lives packed with so many responsibilities there's no time to play. Yes, as an adult you can play. You should. How you define play is up to you. It could be playing games, visiting with friends, running, even coloring in one of the dozens of adult coloring books out there. When you take time for yourself, you are valuing yourself. It's only natural to value others, too.

Charity

WHEN I WAS A KID, I often heard "we don't take charity," which meant our family did without needed clothes, food, even livestock feed. Part of the reason my family had such strong feelings about it was the negative judgments they expected from others and the strings that usually came along with the gifts. The judgment was if you were in need, you did something wrong to be in that position. The strings usually involved religion. If I give you a can of Fava beans that went unused in my cupboard for the last six months, it should buy me points in Heaven and convince you to convert.

I volunteer at an animal shelter, and it is laughable what people give us and take a tax donation for, such as items that are falling apart and have no practical use for the shelter. As a lead volunteer pointed out, if it wasn't good enough for your home, how would it benefit us? Often, we offload out-of-date and broken items that cost charitable organizations time and money to sift through and eventually dispose of. If it isn't good enough for you, then why would someone else want it?

There's a big difference between downsizing and getting rid of what isn't needed than donating items that serve no purpose. The very word *Charity* is often used for *Love* in the New Testament. Love in its simplest form just is. It doesn't question if you are deserving of an item. It doesn't have any expectations of being paid back in any form.

Project Heifer is an organization that helps impoverished families by giving them livestock and teaching them how to raise them. This gives the families an income stream. Many of these families are in third world countries. I've always been a supporter of them and would often give my mother a card that said something like a flock of chickens were given in your name. Even though it was meant to help, she'd be irritated with me since I could have sent people a hundred Bibles with the money I spent. Starving people probably aren't interested in reading.

If I give someone a gift in hopes of getting something back such as a conversion, it's no longer a gift. It's a business deal. It's wrong to assume that those who don't embrace your faith have none. It's also a great deal to expect someone to give up everything they were brought up to believe because they were handed a chicken or a Bible. Anything not given in love is not a gift.

Unfortunately, some people don't see the strings they attach to charitable gifts. When I left my abusive husband, my three children and I were without any income for a short time. Social services couldn't help with immediate needs because that takes about six weeks to kick in. Someone suggested I visit this church that had a food pantry. I'd worked food pantries and had delivered food baskets in the past where there were no questions about need or counties. Even though I had been raised with "I don't take charity," I humbled myself with hopes of getting a cardboard box of miscellaneous canned goods. Instead, I experienced what had to be one of the most humiliating experiences in my life.

There was a line of desperate people waiting at the church basement door, a clerk took information about the family. Each person had to wear a large cardboard number sign around their neck that identified how many people were in the family. We had to push a small grocery cart with wonky wheels to different spots in the room. At each spot, a person would be standing with whatever food item they were in charge of distributing. After giving you the once over, they would place the item in your cart and say the name of the church and "God blesses you." After making a handful of stops and getting about enough to make two meals, I swore I would never do that again. The judgment was so thick I could have worn it like a coat.

When you give something, be anonymous if possible. Do not expect anything back. When I was a kid growing up, times were often hard, but it was most noticeable at Christmas. Some very generous folks came together and bought everyone in the family presents, often practical ones, with some toys and candy for the kids. Back when people did not lock their doors, their plan was to put the presents under our tree, but our dogs foiled that plan. Some were even dropped in the snow as they reversed down our driveway. I never forgot that pure act of love.

We should all be charitable people. Tony Campolo, an evangelist, once pointed out that he did the math. There is enough food, water, and wealth for everyone. No one had to go without. Children don't have to die from starvation. We are the pipeline. If you have two coats, but you never wear one, give it away.

Once we give a gift, we have no ownership of it. Everyone has had that relative who searches the house for the gift they gave you. A few may even take it back if isn't used in a manner they like. Don't be that person. It will not serve you.

The Burden of Stuff

ANYONE WHO HAS WATCHED AN episode of *Hoarders* knows that too much stuff can endanger your physical life. Buddha teaches that stuff doesn't mess you up. It's more about how you feel about it. This is also referred to in Scripture as the love of money is the root of all evil. Notice, it isn't money itself. People can be rich and spiritual, too, but it all depends on how they use their money. There are millionaires, even, billionaires, who run charitable organizations. On the other hand, there are many who don't.

Let's look at the stuff issue. Once a year, I try to clean out my closets and get rid of what I am not using. If I haven't used it in a year, I'm not going to and I send it on its way with blessings that it can be of use to others. There are many options for handling what you don't use. I take items first to my women's group and see if anyone wants it there or knows someone whom it can benefit. Depending on the item, I can leave it with the women's shelter, animal shelter, or Disabled American Vets. While some people sell their extra stuff in a yard sale or online, I don't. The reason is it would give me too much of a time to reabsorb the stuff back into my life.

Since I grew up very poor, having lots of stuff I don't use makes me feel wealthy. It's ridiculous when you think about it. The items could be useful to someone else. If it is something broken, I could salvage the item for usable parts. My grandmother and mother would cut buttons off old shirts before turning them into cleaning rags.

Often stuff gets in the way of relationships. A car I was following had a bumper sticker that read *whoever dies with the most toys wins.* It doesn't make them any less dead. Then you have the surviving family members vying for ownership of the toys. Many families have been torn apart because of family drama over how a family estate was divided. It never ends well. Cousins aren't talking because one cousin received grandmother's pearls while another one got the ugly brooch.

The real problem is we give stuff more value than it deserves. We often take our personal worth from what we own than from who we are. Folks living in a McMansion feel superior to those living in an apartment or a modest ranch. Many who won lotteries and were married often end up divorcing. Sometimes, they argue over how to spend the money. Other times, they feel as if they could do better than their current spouse. It wasn't the money itself that ruined their lives but how they treated it. Others have come into money and treated it logically, often paying off their house, school loans, car loans, and taking a nice vacation before donating most of the remainder to charities.

How important is something to you? Are you a hoarder? Are you keeping it because it is valuable? Do you want to give it to your children? Are you keeping it because it belonged to your children? It's time to examine your attachment issues.

Have you used it within the last year? If you haven't, get rid of it. When you did use it—did you feel good about it? I have a London Fog coat that I wore once in the past year. I'm not especially fond of how it looks on me. It brings me no joy. It's time for it to go and bring joy into someone else's life.

How many do you need of one thing? I moved into a hoarder's house. The bank took it back due to non-payment. The neighbors told me when the people left, they had pulled all sorts of things onto the lawn and porch unsure what to take with them. They eventually got into their vehicles and drove away leaving stuff strewn across the yard. The neighbors gathered up the junk and put it in their extra trash cans for garbage day. There were thirty-eight full trashcans lined up in front of the hoarder house and no one had even entered the house to gather more stuff.

When we started cleaning the house, we had a large dumpster brought in for trash, including the eighteen Christmas trees we found in the attic. The dumpster, which was supposed to hold a metric ton, was emptied twice. What we discovered was the former occupant bought the same item again and again. Many items were still in their sealed packages. Hoarding leads to you not having a clue about what you do have. We found several unmatched single shoes. It made me wonder what they hoarders did take with them.

Hoarding can be financially expensive. It also keeps you from having human relationships, too, since so much time is put into your stuff relationships. Non-hoarders are often freaked out by stacks of magazines and Styrofoam trays that might have use, someday.

The best way to handle this is to seek help, not only for cleaning but to discover why you need to hoard. Sometimes, it is a way to insulate yourself from pain. When you get rid of the excess, you help yourself and others, too. People will be more willing to visit and there is a good chance that you'll have more opportunity for positive relationships.

Are you keeping something because it is valuable, but you will never use it yourself? If it is valuable, sell it or give it away. There are countless collectibles that people were told would increase in value, but never did—such as Beanie Babies. If it is hidden away somewhere or up on a high shelf collecting dust, it serves no purpose. If you intended it for your children, give it to them now, and spare them the family squabbles. It might turn out that the children never wanted it. Don't be upset if they get rid of it. A gift doesn't come with strings.

Have your children moved out years ago and left behind a room of stuff? If they haven't come back for it then, they don't want it. Inform the children of your plans to get rid of it. Give them a date and do so, even if they don't come for it. Sure, there may be some grumbling, but if it was important, they would have taken it with them.

The less stuff you have, the freer you will be. Those who have an embarrassing amount of stuff worry about people trying to separate them from their possessions. Even though they have plenty, they refuse to share. This attitude stymies spiritual growth. Even those who have a modest amount of stuff can still be obsessed with having more and guarding what they have as jealous as a dragon guarding its hoard.

Those who have an open hand policy as far as stuff usually end up having enough to get by. The universe rewards those with a generous spirit. Ironically, generous spirits do not surround themselves with things. Divest yourself of items that don't serve you. This can include attitudes, too. Leave behind your belief that wealth makes you powerful or superior. Remember the person who dies with the most toys still dies. Do you want your legacy to be that you spent a great deal of money in a self-indulgent fashion or would you prefer to be called a generous soul?

In my life, I had moved twenty-two times. Each time, I left stuff behind. Most of the time, I gave it away. When I did, I realized I didn't really need it but was only hoarding the items.

Stuff comes our way through a variety of methods from purchase, gifts, found items, and inheritances. Our mistake is the belief we are supposed to keep everything. It is best to pass on the item when we find someone who has need of it.

After several decades on this planet, I do realize health is a real blessing, as is love, happiness, and compassion. All the rest is just stuff.

Having less stuff will make your life simpler. Giving out of love will bring more love into your life.

Stay Positive

MOST PEOPLE WOULD RATHER BE around an upbeat person than a negative one. That even includes yourself! Ever wonder why positive people have seemingly better lives than negative folks? Did the good life come first, then they decided to be happy? Just the opposite.

Many celebrities dominate social media and entertainment shows with their bad behavior, whiny attitudes, and temper tantrums. Even still, most of the population would view the celebrities as having it all. They have fame, looks, and money. From their love lives being broadcasted over a half dozen mediums, it's obvious they had or have love. So, why aren't they happy?

The target keeps moving for them. At first, it may have been enough to be in a movie, then it must be a blockbuster, before long they want to be declared the best actor ever. So, how does a person stay positive?

Focus on the good in your life. Everyone has something to be grateful for even if it's simply being alive. Be outspoken about the good in your life, but not in a braggy way. There's a big difference between saying it's a glorious day than I'm the luckiest person in the world to be experiencing this glorious day. The last almost sounds like others don't have permission to share in the sunlight and the flowers.

Another great way is to focus on the good in others. Notice when someone does a good job or has a new haircut. People love attention, especially when it is positive. Unfortunately, most of what we hear in our lives is negative. We're told in so many ways how we don't measure up. My grandmother drew people to her like a magnet. She never had a bad word to say about anyone. People could feel at ease around her, never fearing criticism.

When someone tries to imagine their worst critic, most don't imagine themselves. Usually, it is, even if we are only repeating mentally negative comments that have been said to us in the past. Being negative tears us down. When trying to develop a new good habit, negative reinforcement, such as telling yourself you destroyed any chance of losing weight because you nibbled on a donut in the break room, will cause you to stop trying.

Positive reinforcement makes you keep trying. It can be as simple as observing you did eat the donut, but you'll exercise more to counteract the calories and begin anew the next meal.

By stating what you want in a positive way brings it to you. A woman who states there are no good men left in the world doesn't meet any. When she changes her outlook to there are tons of great guys out there and she is deserving of meeting one, she does. This can apply to anything from your finances to your career.

Often, it helps to put your positive intentions and affirmations into writing, then post it where you will see it daily, such as on the mirror. We become what we say. Words have power. Our subconscious mind focuses on the words we use and does its best to make them a reality. Be careful what you say because you are creating your reality with every thought and word. Stay positive.

Learning from the Past

SO MANY OF US LIVE in the past, although we might not describe it as that. Those of us who've been hurt by others often hold onto the pain in the belief it will somehow protect us. Because of that residual pain, we often insulate ourselves from others. We let those who inflicted the pain, either real or perceived, be a major part of our lives if it is only in our minds.

Holding onto the pain keeps the abuser a major player in our lives. One of the first things you must do to let go of the past is to quit blaming yourself. It happened. If you were a child, you had no prior knowledge and were unable to stop it. This could be true as an adult also.

Counseling can be useful to unlearn these habits. This requires a licensed, reputable therapist, and not every therapist will be a good fit for you. Part of the growth process is being able to specify the type of counselor you need. If you were abused by a male, then you might benefit from a female counselor.

Many people who had a bad marriage take the traits of their former mate and superimpose them on whoever they meet, or even dislike people because they have some of the same traits as their exes, including hair color or liking the same sports team. Some might think of it as a way of avoiding similar pain. They also miss out on discovering new friends and fun.

When you emotionally relive an event in your past, you not only bring up the pain from that time but also increase it with each rehearsal. Occasionally, an event which could have been minor becomes much more hurtful than it originally was. It's hard to let go of the past. It does take practice, rather like meditation.

Decide first what you learned. Were you easily fooled by a handsome face? Trusted a person despite the red flags? Were you someplace where you couldn't get help? Decide what you need to learn, then let it go. If you hold onto the memories, it stops you from growing both emotionally and spiritually.

Occasionally, it is good memories of a well-loved spouse, parent, or child that bonds us to the past. Especially at the time of a recent passing, it is hard to believe there is a future. Your memories, photos, and special mementos will be with you.

Statistically, people are sympathetic when you have had a loss in your life for up to six months. Some folks don't even last that long. It's probably when you constantly talk about your departed one, it excludes most everyone else who didn't share the memory. It also keeps you firmly rooted in the past where no one in the present can go. Enjoy the good you have had with your loved one, then let go. It doesn't mean you will forget them. What you will do is not make your loved one the topic of every conversation.

Often people allow their past to dictate their future. Perhaps a person who wasn't a great student assumes they won't be able to learn new skills. They are allowing the past to govern not only their present but also their future. Students who were labeled special needs early on often performed below their capabilities. Once they discovered their capabilities were like others, many went on to college. They overcame their past.

Too often, we allow what we view as past mistakes to limit our life. If a person isn't good at something, he or she assumes it will always be so. None of us are born knowing how to do anything. We learn.

Life is full of changes and lessons. We can learn from the past, not only about the events and the people in them but about ourselves. Instead of bemoaning that things will never be the same, accept they won't be, and it isn't a bad thing.

Holding onto the past involves hauling around emotional baggage. This baggage makes it hard for people to form new relationships or try new things. Most everyone has met someone stuck in a fashion time period. This person continues to wear clothes and a hairstyle forty years out of date because that time period was when he or she was most happy. While anyone should be able to dress how they want, there should also be the option of picking from a variety of styles for aesthetic reasons as opposed to trying to hold onto a moment in time.

Besides not growing, if a person holds onto the past, they block out others. Even though people do care about the person who holds onto his or her past with both hands, it still makes social interaction awkward. They often don't know how to respond and eventually end up drifting away.

Failure to accept the present happens a lot in older people who want everything to remain as when they were younger. The danger behind this is everything that is current is somehow the enemy or bad, including young people. Be able to embrace the life you have lived with its happy moments, its downswings, and the lessons learned. Be proud of your age. Many have not had the privilege of living as long.

Spirituality

"I'M NOT REALLY RELIGIOUS. I'M more spiritual," is a common refrain, but what does it really mean? It's about the same as asking what *beautiful* or *normal* means to different people. You'll get several different answers. So how is spirituality different from religion or are they the same? They aren't.

Many deeply spiritual people are not members of organized religion. However, they do have daily practices such as meditation and living in the moment. They also may interact with nature, recognizing the essence of each creature and living thing.

Science has measured the calming effect of nature, especially water. It's no wonder desert-locations have so many fountains. People are drawn to water in an instinctual manner. The most beloved sounds include a babbling brook and ocean waves. It's no wonder individuals find being near water as cleansing.

In a busy New Delhi airport, the local monks have created a shallow pool with water lilies and a gentle, flowing fountain for harried travelers to relax. The weary airline patron sits on the edge of the pool and puts his feet in the water. This can be a very spiritual experience if a person allows themselves to be in the moment and connect with the healing vibrations of the water.

A truly spiritual person doesn't recognize one religion to be better than another. Instead, she can accept that everyone has their own path. Even though many religions teach that converting people is a duty, a spiritual person will share his or her practices when asked but will never claim the moral high ground.

It is not surprising that spiritual people can love themselves and those around them. They see themselves as being enough and often the carrier of a divine spark. They see that divine spark in others. It is rather like the word *namaste* that is uttered at the end of yoga class, which can be translated to mean the light in me recognizes the light in you.

Spiritual people can be involved in a traditional church, too. They may have been brought up in that faith but have deviated from the black and white doctrine. Instead of trumpeting their personal epiphanies, they may keep them to themselves until they find a like-minded person.

A spiritual person tends to be more of a seeker, also. They will read various books on different religions, visit different religious institutions, and travel to sacred sites such as the vortexes in Sedona, Arizona. Instead of having their mind firmly made up on how things are, they are learning and weighing how certain beliefs would work or not work for them.

You'll more likely hear a spiritual person say things such as, "Nature is my cathedral," "Of course, animals have souls," or "We must have met before in a past life." There are those who make a point to ridicule people who make such statements because they are labeling folks as *Us* and *Not Us*. The *Not Us* people have to be wrong because they think differently. It threatens those who are not spiritual because it causes the tiniest cracks in their belief system that they can only salvage by labeling the *Not Us* folks as bad or crazy.

It could also be a fear reaction to there will soon be more *Not Us* people according to the Pew Survey. The highest regular church attendance is among the oldest Americans and is at fifty percent. Among millennials, it is almost half that number.

So, take a moment and decide if you are spiritual or religious. You could be both.

Religion

EARLY MAN TRIED TO EXPLAIN his world by creating powerful gods and goddesses who oversaw things. It helped him make sense of natural phenomenon he didn't understand and eased his fears. Rituals were created to both honor and call on these powerful, unseen forces for assistance. At first, these unseen entities may have been a uniting force among small roaming groups.

They attributed both good and bad fortune to the unseen entities. A few members of the nomadic tribes rose to prominence by assuming a role of priest or priestess, claiming only they had the ability to communicate with the holy ones.

Communities developed because agriculture drew people together. When this happened, the people sometimes discovered their deities and rituals were not the same. Usually, the religion who had the most followers dominated, often driving out those with different beliefs. However, many Asian and Native American communities were more accepting of different deities and varied worship rituals.

The privileges the holy men or women enjoyed did not go unnoticed by aspiring leaders. They united with the religious leaders, who conferred on them the divine right to rule. This uneasy partnership with religion and government continued throughout history.

In Egyptian history, each pharaoh would ascend to power, and in doing so would raise their own favored god or goddess to prominence. To do so, they often had to use smear tactics against the current favorite. It was more of a whispering campaign where rumors would be spread about the soon to be disposed of god or goddess while the pharaoh's favorite would have grand tales about saving mankind told. This type of religious shift with the change of a ruler escalated in some countries to kill all those who didn't share the same religious preferences.

Many kings and queens made laws that their people could only have one religion. By converting the entire populace to the same religion, the leader could issue laws declaring they were God-given and had to be followed or risk eternal damnation.

King James, who was both a tyrant and unstable, had the Bible changed to reflect his views. The Bible has been changed several times since with councils meeting to either add or remove scripture.

Countless leaders have used religion to declare wars and genocide. Religion is a man-made construct that served people at one time. It became twisted when people used worship of a divine source to judge others. Those who weren't of the same religion were labeled soulless, which made them much easier to kill without remorse and steal their property.

The Abrahamic religions developed the idea of hell to condemn those to everlasting torment who were not of the same religion or didn't observe all the religious laws. Ironically, the Jews used to worship many gods and goddesses, while the Levites were the ones who decided on one god and the male priesthood.

The sacred calf the Israelites created didn't make sense to the average Christian. They didn't understand why a cow merited a statue. It was a symbol of both Hathor and Asherah, the latter was God's wife and eliminated from the Bible. However, she's still mentioned eighty times, which means she must have been all over the scriptures. Both Hathor and Asherah were nurturing, loving deities, which may have been what the Israelites wanted at the time. Both Asherah and Hathor shared the cow as a symbol of nurturing, sustenance and motherhood.

Most religions are simply loose adaptations of those that came before. There are over twenty-seven virgin birth narratives including Buddha, Krishna, Horus, and Jesus. Some people like to think that each time it was Jesus, and he took a different form to reach more people. Many people believe Buddha reincarnated into Jesus, too. It could have happened or not.

While religion has been used to slaughter and control people, gentler souls employed it to help the poor and orphans. Although the Westboro Baptist Church is always making a spectacle of itself with its hate-filled protests, there are nuns, rabbis, and shamans as well as laypeople who lock arms and walk together for equality for all.

Religion doesn't have to define us. On social media, I see plenty of profiles where the person lists Christian, Catholic, or even Hindu as first in their profile. It's almost like they're afraid if they don't do it, they will get a failing grade on their religion report card. It is also a way they only connect with other like-minded people.

When a person only associates with those of the same faith, only attends religious schools, and listens to media that enforces that view, they are participating in basic brainwashing. Children who have been indoctrinated in such a manner are often prey to those who would abuse them within their faith community, assuring them it is the will of God. We now have thousands of court cases of religious officials who misused their position.

Religion tends to be more about behavior than a connection

with the divine. If you do all the right things, you might make it to Heaven. Surprisingly, those who share a pew on Sunday mornings, may not follow all the church's teachings. They come more out of habit than anything else, while others it may be the keystone of their existence.

Churches, temples, mosques, and synagogues were some of the first places people gathered together. The church social often gave young people a chance to meet each other. In a way, it served as a free dating service. Various churches help their communities by donating food baskets and handing out filled backpacks to students starting school. Many people find comfort in the familiar rituals.

In Betty Eadie's book, *Embraced by the Light,* she explains her near-death experience. She asked her guide on the other side why there were so many religions. The guide's response was because the people were at so many different growth levels. A young soul needed everything to be very black and white. With that in mind, there is no right or wrong religion. It's just where you are on the growth spectrum and how you use your religion.

Does My Dog Have A Soul?

MANY MISSIONARIES WHEN THEY FAILED to convert someone, declared the person was soulless. I'm not sure what proof they had to back that up. The declaration failed to take in differing cultures. Not only did they expect to convert the tribesmen, but they also expected to assimilate them into the missionary's culture. When the Mormons failed to convert the Native Americans, the original residents were labeled soulless and avoided as much as possible. It was okay to kill them, too, since they were deemed soulless.

It is easy to see throughout history that humankind labeled each other soulless. This also equates to not being worthy of eternal life. Aristotle believed women were incapable of love and were little better than animals. In some cases, necessary animals such as horses got a little higher standing than human females.

If the ability to love is how we determine if a person or animal has a soul, then dogs have it hands down. Most people have experienced the joy of being greeted by an excited dog when they returned home. Puppies share their enthusiasm for life with everyone they meet. How many people do that? Yet, the dour humans are considered to have souls.

One of my dogs, who passed, demonstrated the most unconditional love I've ever seen. It would be easy to love someone who fed him and took him for walks. What was infinitely harder was to love an older dog that resented him and constantly bullied him. As the older dog's senses failed her, the boxer, who had been the much-resented pup, became the caregiver. He would gently guide the ailing dog to the house with gentle nudges. He'd also stand in front of her for protection if other dogs approached.

I caught the boxer opening the kitchen cabinet with his paw and taking a pig ear from the bag of treats. He carried this to the blind dog. When she couldn't reach it, he pushed it forward. She tried to chew but couldn't with her aging teeth. The boxer took it back, chewed it enough to soften it up and pushed it back to the elderly dog who snapped it up.

Would any person be capable of such selfless love? Would you decide to care for a co-worker who had always been mean to you when her health failed? Probably not. With this in mind, we may need to rethink the animals don't have souls' belief, especially if the ability to demonstrate love is evidence of a soul.

There is comparing people to animals as a negative thing. If you spend any time in nature, you'll discover that animals aren't the violent killing machines they are portrayed to be. Predators kill out of necessity since they are carnivores. Occasionally, animals attack out of fear and to protect their young. Noted author Ted Andrews was raised Pagan and learned to respect and observe nature at a very young age. He also learned that animals appear in your life with messages. Sometimes the message is connected to the attributes of the animal such as it being a loner and nocturnal. Other times it is more about the symbolism we give to the animal such as an owl being wise or whales as keepers of the ancient wisdom. Even though many ancient cultures were very aware of animal interactions, modern societies tend to overlook such things in their hurry-up lifestyles. Andrews chose to write about this mysterious occurrence in his book *Animal Speak.* Animals want to interact with us and not necessarily as the main course at dinner.

Does your dog have a soul? I'd say unequivocally yes. Your dog may have a mission, too. You may be it.

The Giving Planet

AUTHOR AND POET SHEL SILVERSTEIN's much-loved classic *The Giving Tree* details the relationship of a tree and those around it. The tree gives shade and produces apple-like fruit that it gives willingly to all who pass by. At first, this is an unexpected treat, then it is a right. Finally, people scheme how to take advantage of the giving tree. Eventually, it has no fruit to give and is cut down.

The message of the story is simple. Take no more than you need, and there will be plenty for all. The one thing people didn't do in the story was to take care of the tree. They just took what they could get. This allegorical tale was written in 1964, but it could easily be written today.

Nature has so much to offer us. Everyone on this planet enjoys nature's generosity if you're breathing air and walking on the planet's crust. The real question is what do you give back? My Druid friend explained whatever you take you must give something back as an offering or energy exchange. It could be something as simple as a thank you as you pick a tomato or even spit since it is of your body. Your gift could be an action such as picking up trash, feeding birds, or making sure you cut up all those plastic rings that trap marine life.

Most people fail to recognize the fragility of the planet and give back more air pollution via multiple trips in their fossil fuel guzzler. Pesticides and herbicides run-off have created a dead zone where the river meets the Gulf of Mexico. Nothing can live in this chemical soup. There is a trash island in the Pacific that is 600, 000 square miles. That is twice the size of Texas. We created this. We are destroying the giving planet. Many will shrug their shoulders and say there is nothing we can do about it. What a pessimistic and lazy attitude!

Basic manners dictate if someone gives you a gift you return that favor. Every sunrise, every tree, every flower, every birdsong is a gift. Simple changes can have a profound impact. Use daylight whenever possible as opposed to electric light. It will also improve your general health and mood. Walk or bike when possible. It's a win-win for the planet and you. Use public transportation. Plant trees, butterfly bushes, non-hybrid flowers. Non-hybrid flowers provide more nectar for the bees, butterflies, and hummingbirds. Avoid using chemical pesticides and herbicide. Not only will it kill bees, butterflies, and birds that cat them, it has also been linked to learning issues and disease in children due to being in contact with the grass.

There are so many ways you can give back to the planet. You can use products that use less packaging and are friendlier to the planet. Write to companies that have destructive habits, then boycott them. Elect representatives who care about the planet with records to prove it, not the hype they deliver in speeches.

Many of the foods we cherish such as chocolate, coffee, wine grapes, strawberries, and avocadoes will vanish due to the climate shift caused by pollution and environmental assault. Surely the possibility of being without your morning cup of joe might make you decide to vote responsibly.

Our giving planet, just like the giving tree, is exhausted. Instead of assisting the planet or seeking non-fossil fuel methods of energy, our government is prying open parks and wildlife sanctuaries to squeeze out the last drop of oil. While these actions destroy the homes of both people and wildlife, has no one considered what we will do when there is no more oil to create gas for the gas guzzlers?

Will we be a planet of tree stumps, rusted-out cars that no longer run, and hungry people? There will be no fish, no wheat or rice, or fruit. Most of these foods will have disappeared by 2080 or sooner if we don't take the opportunity to give back to the planet.

The Sanctuary of Sleep

ANY PARENT OF A BABY or toddler will fantasize about sleeping through the night. Sleep is that one thing you don't appreciate until you don't have access to it. Those of us in highly industrialized nations are cutting back on sleep and are the worse for it. Our quality of actual sleep is poor, too. We need to sleep for so many reasons. Sleeping habits are directly related to poor food choices.

Most people must jolt themselves awake with an alarm clock, then they stumble into the kitchen for their caffeine starter, which could be coffee, tea, or soda. If they didn't sleep well the night before, they'll eat more and seek out sugary, high carb food options such as donuts. This is because the body didn't fully get to recharge due to lack of sleep. It is similar to the Borgs on Star Trek, plugging into a charging station. When you don't get seven to eight hours of sleep, it is the equivalent of walking around with a half-charged battery.

Over a decade ago, a dear friend of mine confided how he couldn't wait to go to sleep each night. He rhapsodized about getting cozy under his down comforter and drifting off to sleep. What I failed to realize at the time was that he was in the final stages of diabetes. Sleep not only offered him a respite from pain, but it also allowed him to enter a dream world where he was not encumbered by the limitations of his affliction.

Dreaming is important for a variety of reasons. When we sleep, our subconscious is still at work on the problems of the day. Many inventors, scientists, and even authors came up with their life-changing ideas or stories in their dreams. Our spirit guides and ancestors often use dreams to communicate with us. Dreams usually occur in REM (rapid eye movement) sleep, which is the fourth stage of sleep. Noises, lights in the room, indigestion, or being too cold or hot can prevent a person from getting to the REM stage or staying there long. Lack of REM sleep results in memory issues, inflammation, and obesity risk factors. There is also the possibility you are missing out on a message you need to hear.

When I first heard about the necessity of sleeping eight hours, I considered it an impossibility. People have busy lives. What can be given up for more sleep? Television is the first one to go. Since we can watch anything, we want anytime we want, there is no need to stay up late to watch the late show. Most people are now watching late-night talk shows when they get home from work. Computer games or social media shouldn't take up your entire evening. Both have a blue screen which is stimulating as opposed to relaxing. It also makes you hungry. Instead of winding down for the night, a little extra screen time makes you edgy and hungry.

We have rituals or routines that help our bodies prepare for sleep. Even though you might have a big meeting in the morning and need sleep, jumping in bed at midnight with plans to wake up at seven will not do the trick. If you haven't developed a nighttime ritual, it will be hard to fall asleep.

Nighttime rituals need to include no screen time an hour before bed. Your television or phone doesn't come into the bedroom. Studies have shown that having the phone near you can keep you awake with its various notification sounds and lights. It is also a source of radiation that you don't want near you. A few people were so attached to their phones they slept with them under the pillow and caught the pillow on fire. Your cell chirping in the night annoys your partner, too.

An uncomfortable mattress, scratchy blanket, or not having the right pillow can contribute to lack of sleep. Do your research and discover what you need to sleep well. Try out pillows, mattresses, and blankets. I switched out the top sheet for a cozy blanket. Even socks on your feet will help you sleep better.

Getting warm, then cooling down helps people fall asleep. You can achieve this phenomenon by taking a warm bath or drinking a cup of herbal tea. Certain scents such as lavender and rosemary in the bedroom help you fall asleep easier. Soft music or mediation for sleep will produce a relaxed state. Many people will read for fifteen minutes or so before going to bed. It's not the book that matters, but the routine.

Your body recognizes the routine and settles into falling asleep. When you close your eyes, try not to revisit your day. If you do, be grateful for what you have and let it go. Making out to-do lists before bed will allow you to let go of any worries for the next day. Make sure the room is as dark as you can make it. We are diurnal creatures and light triggers us to be awake. Finally, you may want to place some crystals in the bedroom to aid in sleeping. Amethyst, rose quartz, and hematite often work well. Put the hematite under the bed, the amethyst on a bedside stand and rose quartz in the corners of the room. The hematite grounds you. The rose quartz and amethyst help you to relax.

Make sure you give yourself enough time to sleep. If you want to sleep eight hours, go to bed nine hours before you need to get up. If you wake up on your own without an alarm clock, you are sleeping enough. The interruption of an alarm clock often sends your dreams fleeing. There are several alarm clocks you can get that get progressively brighter or emit a soft chime. Never discount the importance of sleep in your life.

Signs, Omens, and Visions

IN 2003, A MINI-SERIES NAMED *Miracles* and starring Skeet Ulrich as a disenfranchised priest premiered. The priest would show up in various places that a miracle occurred. His job was to take information on the *miracle* and report back to the Church. Since the priest himself was experiencing a personal crisis of faith, he hoped to find evidence to believe. Along the way he would see signs everywhere on billboards, in the sky, on water towers that read God is now here or God is nowhere. The letters ran together, so it was up to him to decide the meaning. Unfortunately, the show was canceled, leaving the viewer unaware of the meaning of the words or the young priest's fate.

In the Catholic world, the Church decides if something is a miracle. A dying church in a defunct manufacturing town was losing members rapidly, but a generous donor made it possible for the crucifix at the front of the church to be restored by a professional. Maybe the idea was it would attract more members. After the restoration, one of the altar boys claimed that the statue now had its eyes open. The artist showed photos of his finished work to demonstrate he had not painted the eyes opened. If he had, why would no one have noticed for months?

The church took this as a sign and waited for it to be authenticated. In the meantime, several thousands of faithful visited to see the crucifix with the open-eyed Jesus. The Catholic Church decided this was not a miracle despite sworn testimonies and physical evidence. This upset the church members because several claims that had no collaborating evidence had been declared miracles. Why not their statue? They couldn't understand why their changing face of Jesus wasn't a miracle. It was to them.

How do you decide if something is a sign? The changing face of the statue was a sign to the church members. They needed something to rally around to keep their church open, but the archdiocese decides what churches stay open, not the members. Maybe the diocese was suspicious of the statue. The sign wasn't for the diocese, but for the church members.

Signs are extremely subjective. Many can see a sign, but it only has meaning for some or one. In the spiritualist church, while mediums are doing platform readings, it isn't unusual for the lights to flicker. This is a sign that spirits are present. The uninformed person or disbeliever would consider it poor wiring.

Signs are all around us, but we seldom notice them unless we look for them. The appearance of certain animals, numbers, and even smells can be an answer to a question or confirmation that you aren't alone. Certain smells could be associated with deceased loved ones. The smell of baking yeast rolls reminds me my mother is nearby because there is no one in my house making yeast rolls.

An omen is often regarded as a sign something bad is going to happen, but that is not the definition of the word. Instead, it refers to something momentous happening either good or bad. A comet was regarded as an omen that something or someone spectacular would happen. There are comets in many depictions of Jesus's birth. There are also sightings of comets before battles. The omen can also serve as a warning.

Visions can happen at any time. They can be daydreams, dreams, a flickering image before you fall asleep, even while you're doing something such as yoga. Unlike your movie or book visions, they may be very brief and only the image of one thing or just a word. At the time, it may do more to confuse than illuminate. When the time comes that your vision showed, you already know the right decision or person because it has been revealed to you.

One thing about visions is you do not control them. We all have daydreams of great vacations, romantic partners, or possible desired outcomes. A vision isn't something you necessarily want and often doesn't make sense on the surface. What we regard as vision can come from spirits or spirit guides, and the best way they can communicate is by images.

While relaxing at the end of yoga class, I saw a nest with six green eggs in it. I had to break down the symbolism. Eggs represent new beginnings. Green can represent posterity, love, and healing. The nest symbolizes home, security, and new opportunities. The number six can refer to finding your balance. I was looking up at the nest, so it would refer to the future.

An odd little image can be very full of meanings. A dream dictionary can be helpful, but don't underestimate your own instincts. If you love snakes, then a snake in a dream could be a pleasant thing. To others who are afraid of snakes, it could be frightening.

Every day, spirits, spirit guides, fairies, angels, and even our own subconscious is trying to reach us by using signs. Be aware, but not obsessed with seeing signs. A few individuals refuse to take any action because they didn't get the right sign. Go about your life, think things through, and when a sign is really needed, you'll see it.

If you're unsure, ask the universe for confirmation.

Dealing with Your Shadow Self

IN THE UNITED STATES, WE only accept certain traits as okay. The ideal person is an extrovert, organized, upbeat, and in control. This same person never gets angry, too loud, out of sorts, or despondent. He or she is never clueless or confused. Plus, this person never has negative feelings about anyone. Of course, the ideal person is in excellent shape and wears fun, flattering outfits.

Sound like anyone you know? It could be possibly a one-dimensional fictional character in book or movie, but there is no one really like that. No one. Stop beating yourself up because you don't fit this outrageous personality profile.

A slight road rage due to a dangerous driver in front of you puts all your senses into a focused mode to drive even more defensively to survive another day. Staying in a happy mood, singing to the radio at the top of your voice could cause an accident because you didn't pick up on the possible menace.

Some days, we are more reflective. It could be due to confusion, disappointment, or even grief. Reflection is a wonderful tool to understand our world and know how to proceed. It's okay to take time away from everyone. Even though your friends or family might be asking what is wrong with you, you're okay. Take the time to relax and reflect.

If someone or something upsets you, rather than berating your-self, or planning elaborate revenge scenarios, reflect on why you're upset. Often, a person or situation can be a trigger. Create a plan of action to avoid this trigger or simply accept that the situation is troubling. Acceptance does a great deal to ease the mind.

Everyone has angry thoughts. It's not wrong. The tricky part is how you use these feelings. You see someone abusing a dog. You could offer to take the dog off his hands, report him to the humane society, or volunteer at a shelter. It takes your natural anger and funnels it into the appropriate avenue. Firebombing the abuser's house is not an appropriate response.

Our shadow self is the part we pretend doesn't exist. This may be due to the current Christian majority who embrace an all good all the time deity as opposed to the various other deities who have a duality nature. The assumption is Jesus never got down. If you read Scripture, you are aware he got angry in the temple. He was disappointed in Peter's betrayal and is grief-stricken at his aloneness on the cross. Consider that for a moment. He was not happy-happy.

In an episode of the old *Star Trek* series called *The Enemy Within* featured Kirk being split into two versions of himself. One was considered the good Kirk and the other the bad Kirk. It was a simplistic portrayal of the good Kirk being polite, kind, and compassionate. The bad Kirk was driven, aggressive, and often took what he wanted, which meant he disregarded the rights and needs of others.

Interestingly, the good Kirk couldn't make the needed command decisions because he didn't have enough drive. He needed his shadow self to be a whole individual who could command a starship.

Do as You Will

ALMOST EVERY RELIGION HAS SOME type of rule or rules as far as behavior. Most people have heard of The Golden Rule that advises us to treat others as we would like to be treated. Many Wiccans believe that whatever you put out in the world will be returned threefold. This applies to both good and bad energy. Even though these principles are in place, how many people live by them?

Almost every war has had the backing of some religion. Often, the aggressive nation declares that those who are on the disputed land do not deserve it due to their nationality or religion. Warring nations make excuses for their troublesome actions such as promoting it as a way of peace as opposed to a power grab. This is easy to see with nations, but what about smaller microcosms, such as work, school, or home?

Most of us can imagine our workplace as a battlefield complete with generals and spies. Usually, among siblings, there are territorial skirmishes. School includes everything from surprise ambushes to picking one student who serves as a scapegoat.

The creation of scapegoats allows us to blame others for our problems. The original purpose of the scapegoat was to accept the various sins of the Jewish people. The goat was then loosed into the desert to die. Consider the goat had done nothing to earn this fate. The irony of this custom was that it was started by people who in turn became scapegoats wherever they went.

During boot camp, the term Charlie was used to designate any enemy, but I had no real fears that some unknown person from an unspecified country was currently planning a trip to the Midwest to take over my home, family, and possibly my dog. More likely what was happening at that time was some soldier in another land was being informed that the American soldier wanted to destroy his way of life, including stripping him of his religion, murdering his children, and raping his wife. In his story, I was the scapegoat.

Stereotypes serve as scapegoats. My grandmother grew up believing that Catholics wanted to take over the world. She believed the Knights of Columbus Halls were where they stored the weapons. As people, we have a long history of vilifying those who are different. It certainly isn't how we would want to be treated.

Another part of the Wiccan rede is *do what you will, but harm none.* Moviemakers have never taken this to heart with their promotion of revenge sagas. There are huge debates about what is harm. One good example is if you get a new job, then that means someone else didn't get it, which could mean you caused harmed to someone. It is more about intentional harm.

There is a golf game app that rewards people hitting the other person's ball with a few points. I play the game app against people all over the world. It is interesting to see how people handle the decision to hit or not another player's ball. Most do their best not to. While others are gung-ho trying to knock my ball aside, usually forfeiting their chance to win the game. It makes me wonder if the game is a type of psychological experiment. As the other player, I become *Charlie* and must be exterminated at any cost. Sometimes, the other player ignores the whole purpose of the game, which is to get the ball in the hole first. If the player strikes the competitor's ball, he loses their opportunity to sink the putt.

It's this type of simplistic reactionary thinking that has caused issues as long as people have roamed the earth. It certainly isn't the Wiccan Rede or The Golden Rule. I have been on both sides of the playing field.

When I was harassed by a girl that I didn't even know for the simple reason that I had gone out with her boyfriend before she did, I ironically ended up dating the guy again when he dropped her for being unstable. On the other hand, when I hung out with petty people who enjoyed ridiculing others, I lost real friends.

Social media gives us a skewed vision of what truly happens in the world. People usually crow about devious actions, and a few even make YouTube videos that later get them arrested. Others may have more of a difficult time determining what is harmful and what is not. The easy way to do this is to check your gut. Are you having second thoughts or worried about push back? There's a good chance you shouldn't be doing something, then.

As a girl, I was always told not to do something if I couldn't do it with Jesus observing. That made going to the bathroom a little awkward. Why does something if you'd feel self-conscious or even guilty about your actions if observed by a friend or a neighbor? If something goes directly against who you are, then it is best to avoid it.

My personal life rule is when you do bad things, bad things will eventually happen to you. It may not take the form you expect. It's the same as when you do good. When I returned a credit card, I found in a parking lot to its owner, I didn't reap an immediate reward. I did it because I hope someone would do the same for me. Months later, I was shopping with a friend, and I put down a bag containing all my purchases. Somehow, I got distracted and drove my friend home. Hours later, I realized I'd forgotten my bag. When I returned to my shopping venue, it was exactly where I left it. Were the two connected? I like to think they were, but they may have not been.

Doing as you will and harm none applies to yourself, as well. Consider how you treat yourself. Are you quick to find fault? Do you ridicule your actions? Remember your intent is to hurt none and that includes you.

We shouldn't do good because we want a reward, but because we want to help others. The flip side is hatred, prejudice, and revenge hurts both the person doing it and the target. People die every day hating others, possibly even cursing them with their last breath. Don't let that be your legacy.

Sunlight

SUNLIGHT IS VITAL TO OUR mental health. It also has a positive effect on both our physical and spiritual health. Anyone who has lived in a rainy climate or has just suffered through a spate of rainy days realizes the emotional uplift a sunny day brings. Children play a little harder and often louder, invigorated by the sun. Most weekend activities depend on the sun for those who want to work in their yards, participate in a sporting event, or even take a walk in the park. Ironically, even activities that are conducted inside, such as going to the gym, shopping, or out to eat, increase on sunny days because people are more willing to go out. On cold, rainy, even snowy days, people tend to stay home.

Simply stepping out in the sun increases our Vitamin D production. It improves our moods and can often help with depression and cure seasonal defective disorder. SAD occurs in areas where during the winter there is limited sun and the ability to go outdoors due to the weather. It is a type of despondency that is sometimes called the winter blues but fades away with the advent of more sun.

Alzheimer's patients exposed to sunlight had fewer symptoms of depression, agitation, and nighttime wakefulness. Those suffering from depression felt better about their situation after being in sunlight. Walking, playing, or working in the sunlight resets your diurnal rhythm and allows restful sleep without the help of pills. Those who must travel into different time zones can reset their body clock by allowing the back of their knees to be exposed to sunlight in the new location for about ten minutes. The body interacts with the sunlight and finds its place.

Memories recalled in sunlight are not surprisingly happier and brighter. Sunlight helps us lose weight. Scientists compared those who exercised outside to those who stayed in the gym. The outside athletes burned more calories and lost more weight. There is no hard and fast reason why. It could be the increased production of Vitamin D, the improved mood, more energy, or a combination of the three. A big factor was people who exercised outdoors could control their weight better. This could be linked to less screen time. The blue screen found in so many of our electronics and phones has the unexpected effect of stimulating our appetite.

Even though there have been warnings to stay out of the sun or slather yourself with sunscreen to avoid skin cancer, regular exposure to sunlight helps prevent many cancers including prostate, cervical, and breast cancer. It also improves bone health, heals skin disorders, and assists with eye health. Exposure to the sun can lower blood pressure, improve heart health, boost your immunity, and help reduce the risk of getting Type 2 Diabetes.

Employee's attitudes and work performance show a noticeable upswing if they take a short walk on their lunch break. Getting out of a stifling environment may figure into the improvement, but sunlight improves brain activity. Stuck on a problem? Put a little sunlight on it.

What about skin cancer? Ironically, some of the sunscreens are not only dangerous to humans but are killing off aquatic life when folks slathered up with sunscreen take a dip in the ocean. Avoid any sunscreen containing oxybenzone. It is linked to endocrine issues, organ system toxicity, skin rashes, and can make you allergic to the sun.

Some resorts and dive areas prohibit the use of sunscreen with oxybenzone. It destroys coral reefs and diversely impacts areas that depend on tourism and fishing. Coral reefs protect coastlines from storms and remove carbon dioxide from the atmosphere. That one tube of sunscreen not only hurts the wearer but everything else.

Other chemicals to avoid include octinoxate, which has similar side effects that include reproductive toxicity. Homosalate, while having similar properties like the already mentioned ones, makes the wearer more likely to absorb pesticide. It must be a case of like attracting like. It is also a chemical that doesn't break down easily. It will remain in the environment long after it has washed off into the sea.

Titanium dioxide is a naturally-occurring mineral found in the earth's crust. Titanium dioxide is considered possibly carcinogenic when inhaled. It's best to avoid this ingredient in aerosol spray sunscreens, dry powder sunscreens, and SPF powder cosmetics.

There are safe sunscreens, but make sure that they are reef safe, especially if you are planning to visit the ocean. When we make our seashore visit, we should not be polluting the home of marine life.

Back to the topic of sunlight and skin cancer.

My aunt never went outside until after six pm. When she did, she had on a long-sleeved shirt, pants, hat, sunglasses, and gloves. She also slathered herself with sunscreen. She still got skin cancer, which was promptly removed, and she lived several years after that. People most prone to skin cancer are pale folks. They have a two percent rate while people of color have a less than one percent rate. You have a higher rate of getting into a car accident.

Still, wear sunglasses and hats, especially if you expect to be outside a long time. Safe sunscreens are helpful if you get in your ten minutes of unprotected skin.

What spiritual impact does the sun have on us? People have always been drawn to the sun. Many of the early religious practices related to the sun and in turn created sun deities such as Ra, Amun, and Sol. No wonder since the sun allowed early man to see his prey and predators and helped crops to grow. In the winter, early people would light bonfires to call the sun back. The return of long days must have made them happy. Not too surprisingly, Jesus is referred to as the light.

Finally, when we die, it is believed our spirits walk into the light.

Diversity

INFINITE DIVERSITY IN INFINITE COMBINATIONS was Gene Roddenberry's tagline whenever he started talking about his creation, *Star Trek*. He wanted to show people that life could exist in varied forms. Due to a very tight budget, the aliens tended to look very much like humans and usually very attractive humans.

Most people wrestle with the idea of diversity. Many say they want it while their actions prove otherwise. Still, others want to put a stop to diversity in its human form. What would the world be like without diversity? One example of the impact that the lack of diversity has is the monoculture farm that consists of one crop such as corn or soybeans. Growing up, I lived on a small farm. We had a vegetable garden, grew timothy hay, wheat, corn, and oats. On the farm, we had a milk cow, ducks, horses, and chickens. In a nutshell, it was a tremendous amount of diversity and a typical farm of the time.

Occasionally, something could happen to one crop, such as wheat rust or a swarm of grasshoppers. As bad as that sounds, we had other crops to fall back on. When any insect pest arrived, we had poultry that would often eat them as fast as they could. By planting items such as garlic and onions with the other crops we chased away burrowing nuisances. Dogs kept away deer who might want to help themselves.

Cut to a monoculture farm that has a hundred acres of wheat.

The farmer probably used a GMO seed that he was guaranteed would deliver a superior yield. There are no natural deterrents to prevent wheat rust, which results in the farmer having to insure his fields for thousands of dollars. If he or she can't afford it, there is the possibility of being wiped out with one rust occurrence. The sterile GMO seed is expensive and can't be used to produce more crops next year. The field is depleted of nutrients, too. Dangerous chemical fertilizer is then used. It filters into the groundwater that both people and animals use, causing cellular mutations and birth defects. All this for a product that had been proven to be less nutritious than non-GMO seed.

How is this lack of diversity reflected in the human culture? Fear is the GMO seed of choice. There are a few of us left who have lived through the white flight. This occurred around the seventies, depending on where you lived, due to busing. The federal courts ruled that children of all races should have equal education. Before that time, black children often attended separate schools in decrepit buildings using outdated textbooks that the white schools had long since abandoned. To remedy this situation, the school districts started transporting children across the counties to make the schools more racially diverse.

This resulted in thousands of white families fleeing the cities for outlying small towns of mainly white folks. Several questionable academies sprung up, touting they were of the religious nature when their only purpose was to have white children attend school with only white children, which solidified the students' emerging prejudices.

Due to being a child of a single-parent household, I ended up going to the racially diverse public schools. When I met kids, who attended the academies or the suburban schools, they would ask me about the race riots at my school. There weren't any. Apparently, to justify their racist attitudes, parents who did choose to send their children to academies reported regular race riots at the public schools.

By keeping the white children insulated from children of other races, the parents passed on their prejudices. They also increased the fear factor. Even though most people won't admit it, their prejudices are due to fear. They react by pointing out recent arrests of those of a different race as proof they are the criminal element. There is never any mention that most prisoners are white. Those who are afraid react badly. Those who are being persecuted become prey and react accordingly, often striking back with words or fists, then they are vilified. People point fingers and call them vicious animals.

As a teacher, I have worked at Catholic, charter, and public schools. What I noticed is the Catholic students tend to stay with their Catholic friends and date those of the same faith. This isn't true for all.

In public schools, at a young age, children are exposed to students whose nationality, religion, and sometimes language is different from theirs. Young children, while naturally curious, are fairly accepting. Their standards tend to be if you are nice to me, then I like you.

The older a person is, the harder it is to accept diversity. It's not impossible, though. What would the world be like without diversity? In 2004 satirical film, *A Day without Mexicans*, one-third of California's population vanishes when the Mexicans disappear. Many service jobs are left unfilled, along with mid-level positions, and there are no food trucks. Most of the restaurants must close because their kitchen staff was Mexican.

If everyone in the world was the same color, ate the same food, and wore the same clothes, it would be boring. How would we even recognize each other? There would be no need to ever go out to eat since all the food would be the same. No need to travel since everyplace would be similar. Why would people fall for certain people if we all looked the same? Many industries would fail. There would still be war because greed doesn't change depending on your skin color.

Would we fail to recognize other sentient life when we saw it because our view was so narrow? Probably. It's like the *Muppet Babies* cartoon where they blast off to space to find other life. Even though the Muppets are of various hues, they must expect life to resemble them. They stomp all over the planet looking for life. They are followed by rock-like creatures that can move. They eventually leave declaring there was no life on the planet.

Often, we do the same. Instead of declaring there is no life on the planet, we declare an entire religion or race to have no merit without bothering to get to know the people behind the label. Focus more on what we have in common, such as loving our families and wanting the best for them.

When I encounter people, I may disagree with politically, I try to see the good in them. They want clean water, a safe place to live, and food on their table the same as me. Their methods of obtaining this may be different from mine, but that doesn't make them evil. There is the possibility that by being who they are, they're helping me to grow on my soul path.

Without diversity, there would be no spiritual growth. There would also be no fish tacos, which would be inexplicably sad—for me.

Acceptance

NORMALLY, WE RAIL AGAINST THINGS we can't change, such as rain on an outdoor wedding, an IRS audit letter, or possibly rejection from a potential romantic partner. Depending on the individual, he or she may not take any accountability for the unfavorable consequence. Sure, there isn't much a person can do about rain on an outdoor wedding, but the potential bride or groom could make alternative plans in case of rain or pick an area not prone to pop-up showers. Then there is acceptance.

Acceptance is so underrated. Many meditation practices advise those involved in meditation to be aware that other thoughts will often intrude when seeking inner peace. Instead of being judgmental or critical, it is much easier just to accept these thoughts happen. Acknowledge them, then let them go without any judgment. Good advice. Why can't we apply it to other parts of our lives?

Rather than beat up on ourselves for our perceived failings, acceptance views things in a non-judgmental fashion, then moves on. There is a story about a little boy breaking his mother's favorite lamp. He feels horrible about it. The mother sees his distress and decides he has learned his lesson. She tells him they will never talk about it. When he tries to apologize for the lamp, the mother answers with, "what lamp?" Acceptance, while similar, does acknowledge there was a lamp once, but now it is no longer, which is neither good nor bad but simply is.

Non-acceptance allows a person to pile up past grievances and hold onto them. At a former job, one of my co-workers was a very angry woman who resented her divorce and her ex-husband. Any time she had a chance to work it into the conversation, she did. This caused most of the fellow employees to avoid her. Her angry non-acceptance was toxic.

The woman's inability to accept her divorce, and possibly her part in it, kept her from moving on. It also isolated her from other folks who could have been a supportive network. Her anger kept her from grieving and possibly reflecting on the relationship. All relationships teach us something valuable. Knowing this, no relationship is a waste or a mistake. Maybe we didn't like what we learned from it, but it can still benefit us.

Acceptance is about knowing we can't change another person's mind or actions. There are plenty of parents who have adult children who have cut off all contact with them. For some parents, this is a deep hurt that never heals. It bleeds over into the rest of their lives, contaminating everything. Sure, they can make sure the adult children know they are open to communication, but they also must accept this is a choice their child made. Talking about it constantly to friends will only stir up pain. Eventually, people will avoid the parent who obsesses on their non-communicative child. The best the person can do is to live their current life the best they can.

Anyone who holds onto the past can't experience the joy of the now. A divorced friend fixates on her previous marriage and ex-husband. It robs her of current joy and makes her suspicious of future relationships. It also makes her distrusting of her decisions. One casualty of short-lived relationships is people try not to remember the good. By doing this, it allows them to think they haven't lost too much if they view their ex as being all bad. This does not benefit them because they blame themselves for making such a poor choice.

Elisabeth Kübler-Ross came up with the five stages of grief, which include denial, anger, bargaining, depression, and finally, acceptance. They may not occur in an orderly mannered fashion. A person may bounce back and forth between depression and anger. When a close friend died, I kept thinking it was a long, difficult dream that I would eventually awaken from.

My grief stages took longer than I expected. Eventually, I had to acknowledge that I would hurt for a while. At one point, I had to make a choice to move on. There was no bringing my friend back or the life we may have had together. Moving on or accepting that what once was will never be again is often the biggest struggle. Especially with the death of a child or a loved one, people experience guilt at the thought of moving on. Our deceased loved ones want us to have a happy life as opposed to grieving.

Acceptance can cover a variety of situations. As we age, our bodies change, limiting our activity. Most deal with this by complaining. A few will try to update everything with expensive surgeries. Then there are those who accept the changes and move on. An accident could put someone in a wheelchair, changing everything. How the person deals with this unexpected occurrence not only impacts his or her life but the family and friends(lives?), too.

Whoever coined the expression no man is an island got it right. Refusal to accept your place diminishes you but hurts those around you. How can you accept what is unacceptable?

Realize the situation doesn't have to be what you want or even desire. It just is. Acceptance is like love in the aspect that it must be practiced daily. It's an active process rather like the serenity prayer, which reminds us to change what we can and accept what we cannot.

Acceptance doesn't mean doing nothing. Support can come via counseling, journaling, or even talking it over with a support group. Twelve-step groups such as Alcoholics Anonymous is based on accepting your current circumstances but emphasizes the need for support from a Creator Source and a network of friends.

Even though we may accept something, it doesn't mean it will be that way forever. I may accept my adult child ignores me currently, but we could develop a better relationship in the future.

Acceptance is not approval but recognizing what something is. Someone who is in a bad relationship doesn't necessarily want the relationship, but if he or she can accept the relationship is soul-destroying, then it is possible to move forward to change or eliminate it. Many of our issues come from not accepting something for what it is. Instead, we tell ourselves that it is something else, ignore it, or pretend it will change on its own. It won't. When you can move into acceptance, you can see it for what it is and decide where to go next.

The attitude of acceptance can cover anything from emotions and health to thwarted dreams.

Complicated Grief

WHEN A DEAR FRIEND DIED, I went to pieces to such a degree people got tired of my tears and inability to get it together. Aware of everyone's willingness to indulge my grief was ending, I chose to go to counseling where I found out I had *complicated grief.*

Complicated grief does hit hard because it isn't about just one obvious thing. When my friend died, I was initially sad for him because he wasn't all that old. Then I was sad for me because we would never do the things, we'd talked about doing together. I faced life without his clever quips or breaking into song as he drove. I grieved for the future we would not share. Then my current grief resurrected the empty feeling I had at my father's sudden death. It was as if there was a movie playing in my mind, featuring deaths and losses I had known.

Deaths of loved ones or even beloved pets result in a grieving period, which varies from person to person. The death of a child can turn parents against one another, certain the other was somehow partially at fault for the child's death. The parents are struggling to come to terms with what life will be like without the child. Suddenly, their world is full of things they will never do. They'll never see their child graduate or get married. Their marriage will never be the same as it was before. Anything can set off a searing pain from hearing a child's laughter to spotting an outfit in a store that would be perfect for the deceased child.

Suicides are especially hard since those left behind battle with the guilt that they could have done something or at least noticed the signs. Like those who served in the military, the friends and relatives of the suicide victim may feel survivor's guilt.

Most of us will deal with some type of loss in our lives. It could be the loss of a career, a business opportunity, or even a marriage that didn't work out as planned. A decline in health or simply aging is another loss. Each day an elderly person may measure their happiness or lack of it by how little they can do that day. Anything from tying shoes to getting up off the floor without using hands becomes only a memory.

We encounter people who may be experiencing complicated grief in various aspects of our lives. While the grief may not immediately be recognizable on the surface, we can still try to be compassionate to all people. One of the best ways to do this is to allow the person to talk. When my friend died suddenly, I wanted to tell everyone about him because I felt he'd be forgotten. Ironically, people tend not to bring up the subject of departed ones or loss because it will hurt too much. It's hard to grieve without reflection and time.

The person who never gets to talk about the pain keeps the pain, often hidden down deep. It adds to the complicated grief stockpile. The next time something traumatic happens, the griever has an entire laundry list of why he or she is sad. It would be nice if we knew this, but usually, we don't figure it out on our own.

Author Eckhart Tolle mentions in his book, *A New Earth,* that the fight we have is never what we think it is about. A husband and wife could argue about where to go to dinner. On the surface, it looks like they can't choose between pizza or Mexican food. On a deeper level, the wife might be afraid of abandonment and expects it to happen, which results in her setting up scenarios to test her husband. On the other hand, her husband is worried about not having enough control over his life. His father was always bossed around by his mother. He's determined not to let that happen to him. The real problem is we seldom take time to dig deep into our motivations and share what we find.

With complicated grief, you can start to unwind the threads that bind the losses together by taking time to properly grieve. This could involve doing something to create closure such as writing a letter to a loved one who has passed or even to your future self about how it is going to be okay eventually. Closure could come from a ritual the hurting individual designs. It can also come from taking a realistic look at how the future might have turned out if your loss hadn't occurred. It is easy to assume everything would have been wonderful, but very far from the truth.

I eventually did this with my friend who died. We had talked of going to live in the tropics. Serious talk, which resulted in putting in job applications. In retrospect, leaving our families behind would be a major issue. I could see other problems with this scenario when I wasn't donning my rose-colored glasses.

Those who went through a divorce may blame the other partner, but closure can't happen until each person can accept their part in the failure of the marriage. It doesn't mean there is a good or bad person, but two individuals who made a poor couple as well as making each other unhappy. Acceptance that things often don't work out as we would want is a freeing concept that often releases the residual anger.

The second part of the equation is to learn from it. What we don't learn from, we repeat. Take time to reflect on what saddens you. Talk about it and don't settle for the easy cliché answer. Disappointing things will happen to us, but we don't have to be in freefall forever.

If you believe in reincarnation, you knew before you ever took a breath in your current body there would be loss followed by grieving. You also knew that these things were meant to help your soul grow if you learned from them. That's why we must untangle the threads of complicated grief and make sense of it. Otherwise, it will be a life spent only reacting.

Finding Your Joy

MARK TWAIN IS ALLEGED TO have said, "Comparison is the death of joy." I guess it doesn't matter who said it since the sentiment still rings true. When people compare, someone comes up lacking. It could be us or the other person. If it is someone else, should we take joy in their suffering because it somehow makes us feel better about our own life?

Naomi Wolfe in her book, *The Beauty Myth,* discusses how unhappy most western women are about their weight, looks, and life. In her book, she explores a study where women boycott television, fashion magazines, and social media for a month. Those who kept to the boycott found their happiness and contentment rose almost eighty percent when they were no longer bombarded with unrealistic expectations and airbrushed images, they felt better about themselves and their lives.

Ever wonder how your grandparents felt about happiness? My grandmother, who would now be over a hundred years old if she were still alive, answered this question when I proposed it at a very young age. I asked her if she wanted to be happy when she was younger. Her answer astounded me so much that I never forgot it.

She told me she never thought about being happy. It wasn't something she actively went out seeking. Instead, she tried to do the right thing, which included working hard at school and helping at her parents' grocery store.

Often, happiness or joy was a byproduct of living with integrity. It wasn't always front and center. Neither was it loud and obvious. Sometimes, it came as a quiet sense of contentment at the end of the day.

Nowadays, we think joy is more like a six-foot clown with wild hair that we should recognize immediately. Sometimes, we rush through our truly happy moments to get to the next thing. It is reminiscent of kids tearing open presents on Christmas. They discard one gift to get to the next one with the anticipation that it will somehow be better.

Joy usually arrives in the small things, from a happy greeting from your dog when you arrive home to watching the sun set while enjoying your favorite beverage. According to a study in *Science Daily*, experiences make people happier than things. This means a shared walk in the woods or even flying a kite together creates more memories than various goods. Most of the time, I can't even remember gifts I've been given, and I know my husband is the same. What I do remember is places we have gone and things we have done together.

In the age of the selfie and social media, happiness appears to be more about telling others about what wonderful thing you have bought or adventure you have planned. That tends to put joy in other people's hands or even delays your own joy. Will the experience be better if dozens of people comment on it, or will it cease to be a happy moment if no one notices?

There is a photo from years ago showing a crowd that had gathered for an awards ceremony. Behind the red velvet ropes, a privileged few were close to the celebrities as they arrived and stepped out on the red carpet. Only one older woman near the front experienced the event as it happened. The rest were all looking at their cell phones, taking selfies, or aiming their cameras for a shot. One person experienced the moment. The others hoped to relive the moment as they reviewed their photos only to discover what they assumed was a perfect shot turned out blurry or was blocked by a hand or head.

We are relegating our joy to sometime in the future. I've done this, as have others. Many folks have timelines for joy. We'll travel when we retire. I'll change jobs when the kids move out. In the future, when things slow down, is when I can go out west and see the stars. The theme is there is always time. There isn't. I've had friends die at fourteen, twenty, thirty-six, etc. Others have become so ill that travel was out of the picture. They had to redefine what joy meant to them.

Decide what makes you happy. It can be anything from a perfectly brewed cup of tea to spending time with your children. Joy doesn't come in big packages. More likely, it comes in quiet moments.

When we were planning a trip to India and Germany, a co-worker told me the real enjoyment was planning the trip. I didn't see it that way, but that may have been where her joy was. Different things make each of us happy. Some people take pleasure in marking items off a list while others hate the idea of a list. The important thing is don't give away your joy by comparing it to others.

Selfish

IT ISN'T UNUSUAL TO HEAR people complain about others being selfish. Someone shoots in front of you as you approach a grocery express lane with an overloaded cart. It's easy to define that person as a jerk. As a child, you possibly remember your brother or sister not sharing a coveted candy bar. Some animals can even show signs of this annoying characteristic. We had one dog that would rip a treat away from the more submissive dog and gulp it down. Having said all of this, is there ever a time to be selfish?

Yes, there is. We all need time to renew emotionally, spiritually, and physically. Even though Sunday, as a day of rest, may have had religious roots, it is still a good deal for everyone. Do we rest on Sunday? Usually not. It is the day to do yard work, wash clothes, go grocery shopping, or pack the entire family into the car for church. If anyone thinks getting a family ready for church isn't work, then you're in denial.

Everyone needs a rest and recharge period, especially if you're caring for an aging parent, special needs child, toddlers, teenagers, or even a demanding spouse. Due to economic hardships, two jobs become a necessity, making downtime even more inaccessible.

When does the all-important rest period happen?

Me-time can be had in segments when you can't fit in a large block of time. Start out by going to bed earlier. For people who swear they have no time, check out how much time is wasted watching television or on the computer or phone. Even though many may think watching television or playing a video game relaxes, it doesn't.

At lunchtime, take a walk outside. If weather prohibits such a venture, walk inside or take the stairs instead of an elevator. Park farther away from your office and walk. At home, take the dog for a walk, which will always take much longer than you expect. Dogs live in the now and enjoy every second of the walk.

Set boundaries. Mothers relate countless stories of children negotiating deals while their parent is in the bathroom or even coming right in. Early on, children should be taught to wait, unless blood is involved.

Decide before you start something how much time you can reasonably spend on it. When I started volunteering at the shelter, I only wanted to work a day a week. Soon, I found myself sucked into two days, then three, which I couldn't possibly manage with the rest of my responsibilities. Part of setting boundaries is saying no. It will be very hard if you're a people pleaser. Still, you must do it for yourself.

A sense of pride can only happen when you did the best you could. Along with the pride is usually permission to rest and take a break. Do we dash through life preoccupied with other things that we don't even try to make a good job of what we do? It might explain the missing pride or the willingness to take a deserved rest.

What happens if you aren't a little selfish and grab some me-time? It isn't unusual to hear a parent snap at their child in public or even threaten with ripping off their arm and beating them with a bloody stump. While some might assume the parent is a monster, it is more likely the yelling individual is teetering on the edge of burnout. Besides modeling irrational behavior for the children, the parent is emotionally abusing them and on the edge of physical abuse as they yank their child around the store. The parents are too tired to think things out.

Moms and Dads need breaks. Many churches offer a Mommy's Day Out where they babysit for a set donation. Many women and men use this time to go back home and enjoy an uninterrupted nap. Sometimes, you can arrange with other beleaguered mothers to watch each other's children for short periods of time, allowing each other personal time. Don't be afraid to ask for assistance. If someone tells you how they did it all on their own, they're lying.

It is okay to lower your standards. No one needs a three-course meal after working all day. Sandwiches work, especially if you're too tired to cook. Listen to your body. Take time to sit down and breathe. A running magazine promoted the idea of sitting still for ten minutes to see how you felt. If you fell asleep, then that is what you needed instead of running.

While your body needs a break, your mind and spirit do, too. How can you rest your mind? Avoid noise, worries, and conflict as much as possible. It may sound like an impossibility, but it isn't. Turn off your phone. Announce to your family, you are taking *me*-time and don't want to be bothered. Take a bath. Listen to soft music or nature sounds. If you have access to a pool, take a swim, or even just sit by the water. Running water can be very soothing. Many people put miniature fountains on their desk to sooth them. Blue is very relaxing, too. A photograph or picture that features blue and possibly water in your direct line of vision can help you unwind as you take a few deep breaths, often mentally counting to four as you inhale and to five as you exhale. Making the exhale longer helps to relax faster.

As for your spirit, take time to get to know yourself through meditation. This just isn't sitting on a pillow chanting OM. It can be anything that puts you in the zone from coloring to floating in the water. It must be something that puts you in the now. Strangely, beading works for me, although I do enjoy the guided meditations by *The Honest Guys* on YouTube.

Guided meditation allows space for you to hear your inner voice. It also occupies your mind and keeps it from wandering off. Meditation reduces stress and anxiety, helps us connect with our inner self, opens our creativity, and makes us more productive. Plus, it helps to control addictions.

Knowing this, it would be a shame not to carve out *me*-time. I used to be the overworked mother, wife, and teacher. When I decided to take time for myself, my relationship with my family and co-workers improved. When I chose not to do as much, I was able to be more loving. Sometimes, being selfish when it comes to *me*-time, is being thoughtful of everyone else.

Chicken Wire and Worst-Case Scenario

WORRY COMPELS US TO BUY products we don't need. It also keeps us from doing things we want.

Most of us are afraid of looking like a failure or worry about what others think. As a child, I remember my mother shouting at me to close our windows when my teenage sister went into a full out rant. She must have assumed no one in the neighborhood ever had a teenage daughter. My mother worried about looking bad to people we never ever talked to, let alone associated with. Besides, what I knew about their children made my sister's temper tantrums mild in comparison.

Most of our time is spent worrying something might happen from tornadoes to personal rejection. Often, we are victims of self-fulfilling prophecy. Ever noticed how what you fear comes to pass because you dwelled on the very thing? Sometimes, it is even a relief to have it happen because there is no longer the waiting for it.

This may have been the case with the roto-tiller and the chicken wire. Early on, I learned bunnies love gardens. My husband's solution was to wrap each raised garden bed in chicken wire to get the nibblers out. It also made it hard for me to get in and out due to not having a gate, and using the tiller inside the chicken wire was a delicate operation. I usually bypassed corners, not wanting to take a chance of the blades tangling with the chicken wire. I worried about this, even envisioned it happening, and lo and behold, it happened one day.

It only took seconds for the blades to chew into about six feet of chicken wire and wrap it tightly around the machine. My first impulse was just to walk away, but I couldn't. I needed to fix the fence and the tiller. Even with wire cutters, it took a long time to cut my way through the wire wrapped around the blades. As I cut, I mumbled to myself about the chicken wire. It gave me plenty of time to decide what I could have done differently. I could have taken down the chicken wire to plow and put it back up when I was finished. It would have been much easier than cutting hundreds of tiny, twisted sections of metal.

What I learned from that experience was that it pays to have a worst-case scenario, then plan for it, which takes away the worry. Ironically, the worst-case scenario usually doesn't happen because you are no longer obsessing about it and breathing it into life.

Worry is fear on steroids. All it does is make you physically ill and often emotionally paralyzed. The best way to handle something that worries you is to examine it in detail. Is it a legitimate fear? Since I live in a land-locked state, being chased by crocodiles isn't a legitimate fear. Being in a car wreck is. Once a decision has been made on the validity of the concern, plans should be made how to handle the scenario. If a possible car wreck is an issue, be aware on the road, and avoid drivers who appear to be distracted. It might even help to not travel at peak times or in heavy traffic. This isn't always an option. A defensive driving course might even ease fears. Imagine yourself reacting calmly in a worst-case scenario such as a wreck. What would you do? Walk yourself through the various steps with a satisfactory conclusion that does not involve a medical helicopter. This will mute most of the worry voices in your head.

My grandmother was fond of telling me that worry was like an old Plymouth you saw down a distant road. You were convinced the car was coming right at you. Most of the time, it turned or ran into a ditch before ever getting close. Her point was worry is a waste of time. Time spent worrying could have been spent doing something more enjoyable.

Most people would have thought I learned my lesson about the chicken wire, but I hefted the tiller over the fence again only to have an accident of the chicken wire type. Only this time, while I wasn't happy, I wasn't as upset as before because I had already been through the scenario and knew how to fix it.

Compromise

ON THE DEATH OF MY dog, I considered the compromises we'd made to have a dog. We accepted that on any dark outfit we'd be sporting golden brown hair. Even though he had very little white on him, he almost always managed to shed that on my black clothing. I have spent sixteen years of showing up with a bit of dog hair on my clothes.

Compromises extend to children, too. Any decent parent is quick to get their children needed shoes or a winter coat while doing without themselves. When I made the choice to bring a child into the world, I knew there would be sacrifices.

Any good marriage is full of compromises. My husband and I didn't enter the marriage with the same likes. He will often surprise me with tickets to a concert I wanted to attend, but he would have taken a pass on as a single person. My ex-husband thought everything should be about him every hour of the day. He knew nothing about compromise.

Getting through the day without making a compromise or two is hard. At work, due to recent school shootings, security was beefed up. It's additional work just to get through the front door of a public school. As a substitute teacher, I ring the bell, state my name and my business. I am identified via the camera, and the schedule is checked to see if I am supposed to be there that day. The door is unlocked for me to enter. If anyone is sprinting to get in on my door unlock, I shut it fast. For the school to be secure, I must sacrifice being a thoughtful person and holding the door open.

Sometimes, the word compromise has bad connotations. Maybe it would sound better if I used the word indulged. Whenever I drive a certain friend home, she always gives me directions to her house. Never mind, I've been there numerous times. Instead of snapping at her or reminding her I do know how to get there, I smile and think how great it is to have a close friend.

There are many people in the current society who believe compromise is bad. My previous marriage ended because my ex never considered doing anything I wanted to do. If it crossed his mind, via me suggesting it, he replaced it with what he wanted to do. Millennials are having a hard time with commitments because they've been told via the media that their significant other should be everything they want and need in their lives. In other words, he is former navy seal philanthropist billionaire who loves doing nothing better than spoiling his babe.

Our world would be a better place if we all slowed down, realized the people around us are not the enemy and take time to really interact instead of staring at our phones. That would take a great deal of personal compromise. Compromise is composed of the word promise and com. Com's definition includes with and together. Basically, compromise should be with promise or together with promise. It means to work together. Simply put, working together means you can't always have it your way, which is sometimes a good thing.

Trees and Forest Bathing

TREES USED TO BE THOUGHT of as pleasant plants we chose for shade and beauty. The humble tree does so much for us. First, it cleans our air by taking in carbon dioxide and putting out oxygen. It gives us shade, the birds and animals a place to live, and a stable place to hang a tire swing or bird feeder. Studies have shown leaning against a tree, hugging a tree, or even sitting under a tree for ten minutes or more has immense benefit for our mental health.

Japanese doctors have even started prescribing Forest Bathing, which is being in contact with and taking in the atmosphere of the forest. This is hard to do in the crowded cities, which led to parks being built that would provide the forest experience. A person who is partaking in the forest bathing experience doesn't casually jog through on their way to somewhere else. Instead, they take in the forest using all their senses: inhales the smell of the evergreen trees or loamy soil, feels the sturdy soil or even mud under their feet, tastes the freshness of the rain-washed air, hears the crunch of the leaves or the low moan of trees bending in the wind, and throws back their head and looks up into the canopy that the leafy branches make.

The average person spends almost 93% of his or her time indoors. Most people live in cities, too. It's no wonder people are suffering from Nature Deprivation. When people do engage in Forest Bathing, sometimes for as little as two hours, the results are obvious. Their pulse is slower, and their energy increases. Symptoms of depression, fatigue, stress, and confusion lessen sometimes to the point of almost not existing. Forest walkers reported feeling less angry and less sad.

The results aren't too surprising since trees take care of their own. Why not extend that compassion and care to every living creature on the planet? Tree researchers Suzanne Simard and Peter Wohlleben have both discovered the fungal networks trees use to communicate with each other and at times feed one another. Seedlings often flourish in the shade of much bigger trees without sunlight to create food. It's been discovered that the older trees are feeding the younger ones.

The trees also communicate danger, such as wildlife feeding on them, fire, or even sickness or a logging crew. Some trees can put forth bitter tannins to make their leaves bitter, while acacia trees emit a gas to scare away the leaf-eaters. Peter Wohlleben, who now maintains the beach forest, found a stump from a tree that had been cut decades ago that was still being pumped full of chlorophyll via the other trees.

Trees of the same species tend to look out for each other. Other species may make alliances to keep the forest healthy. Trees don't need to be thinned out. The forest will take care of itself if allowed and can help other species, too. It makes those talking trees in The Wizard of Oz much more believable.

Next time, you walk through the forest and think the trees are whispering, they are. Spend time with them. It might make you think twice before casually breaking off a branch.

Duty vs. Compassion

ON THE WAY TO SEE an ailing relative, we passed several white vans filled with teenagers. They had signs on each of the vans to identify them. When we reached a rest stop, we met up with the vans whose occupants spilled out with glee. They were part of a church mission group headed to Appalachian. I wondered what they would do there, but I didn't ask.

I had been part of the church youth group program and had chaperoned more than a few. As I remembered the scenario, all the youth were expected to go on the annual mission trip. It was what we did to honor God and get the church some good PR as a happening place. There was actually very little compassion involved. Instead, there was some excitement about being away from parents unless your mom chaperoned. Sorry about that, kids.

It was an opportunity to spend time with your friends. Ironically, there were more than a few hookups on the trip, too. It all depended on who organized the trip and its purpose, if anything, was learned by the youth. One trip consisted of going to Mexico City to teach Vacation Bible School. Not a kid and hardly a chaperone on that trip could speak Spanish. The Mexican children were not interested in VBS. They all were solidly Roman Catholic. They must have wondered why this bunch of Anglos were even there. As some type of penance, it was a duty trip to guarantee a Heavenly reward. In other words, it was all about the individual's possible reward, not graciousness or compassion. The parents and youth minister advertised it as a Godly vacation, too.

In a landlocked state, it's easy to dismiss victims of the hurricane until we went on an actual aid trip. No one set up Bible studies in tents for people who had been victimized by the hurricane, then later by scam artists. Instead, we worked pulling off damaged drywall, repairing roofs, picking up trash, and painting. Instead of colorful Bible handouts, the group came with supplies to rebuild homes. Evangelizing was put aside for hard work and occasionally offering a shoulder to cry on. The second trip was more about compassion. There were adults with expertise in carpentry and home repair who instructed the youth. Not only did children learn the damage a hurricane wreaked physically and emotionally, they also learned the value of a case of water and a helping hand.

There's plenty of opportunities for mission work. Volunteering with a compassionate heart does so much for our communities and us. It helps us connect to other people. It peels away the rhetoric and allows us to meet the real people behind hard situations. The very act of helping others, be it visiting the forgotten elderly in a nursing home or working in an animal shelter, gives purpose to our lives. It makes the volunteer feel better about him or herself.

You learn stuff. Sure, you get the story behind the story, but you also develop skills. Think of all the people who learned basic carpentry skills by working on houses for Habitat for Humanity. Even though I've owned dogs forever, I've still learned valuable information for caring for my pet by working at the animal shelter.

Volunteering can be more effective than popping a pill for anxiety, stress, or depression. It increases happiness, self-confidence, and social skills. It also combats loneliness by connecting you to others. Those who volunteer stay in better health and tend to live longer.

Still, many volunteer because their job or school requires service hours. It's easy to pick those individuals out. They complain about everything and quit as soon as they meet their basic requirements. I doubt they receive much benefit. The other volunteers were probably relieved to see them go, too. Some of them may have started volunteering out of duty, but it morphed into compassion.

I try to believe that no matter what a person's attitude is, if he or she is doing something beneficial, some good will come out of it. There's a big difference between blaming a person for being in a sad situation and empathizing. Most people want a hand to help them up and not a handout. Be that helping hand and compassionate heart. Be the change the world needs.

Feathers

EVER STUMBLE ACROSS A FEATHER, even inside? A few people take it as a sign from an angel, a dead loved one, or that the universe has your back. There is even a color system for determining what the feather means.

White is usually an angel is near. Pink is someone who loves you is thinking of you or possibly someone with a pink boa recently passed by. Purple is connected to the third eye and represents the spiritual side. It could be your spirit guides are trying to get your attention. Red is for the crown chakra and strength. Yellow feathers represent happiness. Black and white feathers are for change. Green is lucky and means fortune favors you. A blue father can be a sign of healing and communication while a grey feather can represent peace or be a reminder that things aren't always what they seem. Brown feathers represent grounding and stability. Surprisingly, black is a sign of protection that repels negativity. Orange stands for creativity.

Ironically, if you are finding feathers outside, most of them will be grey due to most common birds having grey feathers.

Feathers can be natural or man-made. The important thing is they occur where no feathers were before, and you notice it. If someone else sees the feather, then the message was for them.

Many folk tales feature feathers from pointing out a liar to giving a shy child confidence.

The feather isn't the magic, but a symbol of the magic. If you spend all your time looking for symbols, then very little will get done. Ted Andrews mentioned he was driving to a presentation and was looking for animal symbols and was disappointed when he found none. Afterward, he saw raccoons lined up along the road as he drove by. His symbol or confirmation came later, not before.

Often, we wait for the perfect symbol or feather to fall directly into our path. It would be grand if that did happen. Every one of us has intelligence and intuition. Intelligence allows us to research the situation, hopefully without too much emotional overtones. Intuition gives us a gentle nudge with an uneasy feeling that something isn't quite right. Of course, people can meditate, call on their guides, or talk over things with their current friends to work out problems. In the end, feathers can be fun to receive, but we can't stay stuck in place waiting for a sign. Way back, I remember people reading their horoscope before deciding if they should leave the house that day. As you can imagine, that didn't work out well. The horoscope became a crutch or an excuse for inaction. We have all the tools we need to live productive lives. Feathers can be confirmation that we are doing so, a blessing on an ordinary day that keeps us going.

Prejudice

A FIFTEEN-YEAR-OLD STUDENT CAME TO me and told me she needed to drop out of school. My first reaction was dismay, and I inquired why. Apparently, she was pregnant with her second baby. Her mother was already taking care of one baby and refused to take care of another, forcing the young mother to drop out of school to attend her children.

My expression may have been one of horror because she exclaimed, "You're prejudiced and jealous of my love with my baby's daddy."

I sighed. No one wants to be called prejudiced. For a moment, I reflected on the word itself. There are all types of prejudices. Most are based on ignorance and stereotypes. I grew up thinking all tall guys could play basketball and both businesses and many women prefer taller males. The first believes they are driven individuals, which in turn makes them better husbands to the second. Neither assumption is based on fact. There are also bewildering beliefs such as black dogs are more likely to bite you. Wiccans, Atheists, immigrants, and even people of color fall under the heading of people to fear.

Occasionally, a seemingly positive stereotype can be limiting, too. An extremely tall student was pursued by the basketball coach, who pleaded for him to try out for the team. When the student consistently said no, he was given the cold shoulder by the coach and other team members. Nature had given him a definite advantage in a sport that often favored the tall, and he chose not to use it. An Asian student who is bad at math often doesn't get the help he or she needs. Instead of thinking the student has an actual need for further instruction, it is assumed he or she is lazy or faking it. Many con men rely on the clean-cut image as being trustworthy. They go door to door bilking seniors out of their limited incomes while dressed similarly to Mormon missionaries.

We often fear what we don't know. This is exacerbated when we listen to repeated falsehoods by others, often by people who are even more clueless than we are. Sometimes a prejudice can be caused by one bad encounter. When my mother was young, she almost lost an eye to a Siamese cat whose scratches came perilously close to one eye. Not too surprisingly, she assumed all Siamese cats were vicious, eye scratching machines until my sister adopted one who was friendly and had no desire to scratch out any eyes, human or otherwise.

Prejudice can be both a noun and a verb. Most people use it as a noun. As if it is a thing like a sweater you put on. Sometimes, it is a verb showing an active bias. You can be prejudiced against something, also, because you have seen the consequences. This wasn't the first time a female student had come to me and confessed her pregnancy along with plans to drop out of school. Once out of school, it would be no easy task to finish. Even earning her GED could prove daunting. The tests a student must pass to earn a general equivalency diploma are much more challenging than sitting in the classroom. Even after a student earns the rather elusive GED, many potential employers treat it as if it were nothing. They'll hire someone with a GED over someone who is a dropout, but they'd hire someone who finished high school the normal way first, assuming the job applicant has more staying power and was somehow smarter than the GED graduate.

Knowing all this, I was and am prejudiced against girls dropping out of school. I went on to say I was against domestic abuse and people abandoning pets in the country when they grew tired of them. As for being jealous of her love, I didn't even address it.

Even though it was very long ago, I could remember being sixteen and being certain my young boyfriend and I would be together forever. Obviously, that didn't happen. We drifted apart as young lovers do. Years passed, and my definition of love changed.

My student shook her head as I inquired about future schooling. I pointed out there were online options, or she could pursue homebound instruction when coming to school proved too much. After all, she has already been in school for eight years. Why waste it?

My speech earned me a sad look as if I was the one who had somehow got it wrong. If asked, she would probably say she was prejudiced against adults telling her what to do as if they somehow magically knew what was right for her.

While most prejudices are out of ignorance, a few are based on natural caution such as avoiding unknown snakes, growling dogs, or smiling strangers who want to sell you something. A few are based on experience, sometimes your own or possibly others', that can be a valid prejudice—that rare time when it was okay to be against something. At one time, men were very much against women voting. Some still are.

When we come across our own personal prejudice, we need to examine it. Is it based on ignorance or experience? Many people fear or are biased against pit bulls without ever interacting with one. Ironically, I owned a pit mix for almost two decades, unaware the gentle dog was part of a feared breed. Because of my work at the shelter, I met many loving pits and a few abused ones who would growl and snap like so many of the other mistreated dogs. If I held onto my ignorance, I would still be biased against pits.

If a fear such as a natural caution against walking too close to the road because I might get hit serves me, then I will hold onto it. Most people feel more comfortable with the words fear or biased as opposed to prejudiced.

As for my student, she did drop out of school. Because her brother continued to attend, I got news now and then. She had her baby. The young father visited for a few months but vanished when exposed to the challenge of rearing a child while still a child. As far as I know, she never returned to school. Even though most may not have seen it, she had potential and an agile mind. Unfortunately, her undeveloped intellect couldn't save her when she was lost in a sea of hormones and assumed her young lover would rescue her. Too bad her distrust or prejudice against adults caused her to refuse assistance from those who only wanted to help.

Your Ancestors are Calling

A RECENT BLOG ARTICLE RANKED the eighteen best psychic shows. This wasn't all of them by any stretch of the imagination. Most featured a medium. Some of them were low-key with the medium conducting group reads. Others had flamboyant medium stars who opened their home, pets, and cooking skills, not to mention their love life, to the television audience. Many of these shows have a large following. Knowing this, why is it so hard to believe your ancestors are trying to contact you?

Your ancestor isn't just your great-great-grandfather, but anyone who dies before you. Your friends who have passed over and even your former pets may try to reach you. On the other side, time is different, which means your loved ones haven't forgotten you if you haven't heard from them. Often people die unexpectedly. Even those who are terminally ill may be in denial. They die without communicating final goodbyes, resolving differences, or even revealing the hidden location of the buried family silver. It could be they've sent you signs, and you chose to explain them away.

How do you know you're experiencing contact? Most spirits can't manifest a ghostly form or even talk in a normal voice as in the movies. What they can do is mess with your electricity and electronics. Have a flickering light bulb or one that blows for no reason? A television that turns itself off and on, switches channels, or the volume goes up or down without any help from the remote is a definite sign. Many have reported objects such as a radio or record player turning itself off and on.

Signs are often specific to the individual. A hairdresser might communicate by turning on a hairdryer to demonstrate who is calling. A smell can be a sign, too, especially when there is no reason for that aroma. My mother was known for her yeast rolls. No one else in the family could duplicate her skill with bread. Now and then, I wake up to the smell of yeast rolls baking. Unfortunately, there are no rolls, but I know my mother has dropped by for a visit.

Spirits exist on a different vibrational plane. As physical beings, we are warm-blooded and lower vibrational. Everyone has probably seen a version of a ghost hunters show where they experience a cold spot. This could be as simple as goosebumps resulting from a chill, but our ancestors and loved ones do want to contact us. They want to reassure us they made the transition okay. Most of the time, they want to express their love and encourage those they left behind. Every now and then, they have information to relay about future events, but it is hard to get the living's attention.

Music that is somehow associated with a loved one will play or be on the radio when you turn it on. People have reported music playing even when the radio was unplugged or CD players skipping to the desired song.

Cell phones and laptops can be put in use by the dead. They can experience the same off and on issues, even ringing when no one is calling. Some individuals have experienced text messages from the dead person's number.

Waking up in the middle of the night and seeing the same number over and over can be significant. It could be the time a loved one died. Even though most of us don't realize it, we often have close psychic connections with those we love. It isn't surprising for a family member to know another is in distress. It shouldn't be too surprising to know when the same person transitioned from this life.

There are old stories about grandfather clocks stopping when the family patriarch died. Watches and clocks do stop not necessarily when someone dies but as a way of your people trying to contact you. Other times, it can be random things such as a billboard or a personalized license plate that reminds you of a deceased friend. They didn't create the billboard or personalized plate, but they did manage to draw your attention to it. It may not have been the first time they tried to get your attention, either.

The ancient Greeks believed butterflies symbolized resurrection. Whenever they saw one, they believed it was a soul ascending to Heaven. It's not too surprising that an abundance of butterflies or a significant one could be a message from the departed. Dragonflies and hummingbirds can also be a sign from your loved one. To determine a regular butterfly from a message one, watch its behavior. Is it hanging around you trying to be seen? If so, it is a message butterfly. Most people report seeing these visits immediately after death or a funeral. It is a comfort issue. As if the winged creature is trying to convey that the loved one had made the journey successfully.

Does it ever feel like someone touched your hair, hand, or shoulder? Ever see something fall off a table for no reason or something fly across the room as if flung by an unseen hand? This could be an ancestor. It is possibly a younger spirit or even a cat spirit.

Bereaved pet owners have reported hearing dog tags clink in an empty house and the patter of paws. Still others claim their previous pet led them to their current pet. As mentioned before, feathers can be signs, too, and not necessarily of a pet bird.

Other people insist pennies or dimes on the ground are a sign of their loved one because their grandfather or parent always picked up pennies from the ground. Movement or shadows from the corner of your eye can be your relative or loved one. It takes a great deal of spectral energy to achieve the shadow image. People will often feel their loved one is near, especially at significant events such as a marriage or the birth of a baby.

When people used landlines more than they do now, a phone ringing once could be a call from the great beyond. It usually happened when the person was thinking of their loved one, on their birthday, anniversary, or a significant holiday they had spent together.

With digital cameras in our phones, almost every moment is saved on the camera. When photos are examined, orbs may be present. The best way to determine if this is cousin Bob or an issue with your phone is to enlarge the photo. A camera issue will pixel out while a spectral orb retains its shape.

While certain religions frown on having contact with the departed, calling it witchcraft or Satanic arts, most of us know when we have been visited but have a hard time admitting it. It can be anything from the couch cushion depressing next to you or your pet staring at nothing avidly. Small gifts or lost objects can appear on your table when needed. Next time this happens, call out to whoever you think is visiting. This can be aloud or in your mind. Wait. Listen. You just might receive an actual message or simply comfort from the great beyond.

Vegan or Meat Eater

IN THE MOVIE, *SHIRLEY VALENTINE*, the main character is asked to watch the dog of her socially correct neighbors. Instead of giving their bloodhound dog food, they've opted to feed it granola and yogurt. The dog is not a fan. Shirley decides to feed the dog the steak she bought for dinner. The dog gobbles it up because dogs are meant to eat meat.

Should people refrain from eating animals and their animal by-products such as eggs and milk? It's the question Dinty W. Moore, the author of *The Accidental Buddhist*, wrestled with in his practice. Every Buddhist gathering, temple, or retreat he attended offered only vegetarian meals, possibly Vegan, which is the exclusion of milk, eggs, butter, and animal fats. As a respecter of life in all its forms, it seemed like the right thing to do. Later he discovered all the Dalai Lamas ate meat. The reasoning behind this was people were meant to consume protein. It would be like shaming a lion for its desire to bring down a gazelle for mealtime.

As a child raised on a farm and surrounded by my food sources, it made sense to consume the animals we were raising. I will admit my father told us we were eating the hen that always pecked at us or the cow that kept escaping.

PETA, People for the Ethical Treatment of Animals, overlook the most basic issue with sudden worldwide vegetarian turnover. What happens to the animals that are no longer consumed? If chickens serve no purpose, then they will cease to exist. Cows and pigs are too big and expensive to be pets. The domestic species of animals will cease to be. It's not like we will have wild Angus roaming the countryside as bison did centuries ago. The typical milk or beef cow seldom lives past five years of age. Who does funeral detail for these animals? Maybe your community is better than mine, but roadkill is on our streets for weeks until the unlucky animal's corpse is no longer distinguishable.

Basic nutritionists tout the benefits of grass-fed beef and pasture-raised chickens as a clean protein that makes you feel better and weigh less. With that in mind, consider the adage we are what we eat. Do we want to ingest an animal that enjoyed the sun and grass while mingling with its avian friends or do we want to consume meat that was raised in a crowded barn, often in total darkness? Darkness or low light prevents the chickens from pecking at each other or even pecking each other to death. The crowded conditions of cages stress a chicken out.

Milk cows on a grass-fed farm can graze at their leisure. Even the fields are sown with a specific combination of grass and clover to produce the best-tasting milk and cheese. They're exposed to sunshine, fresh water, and air. The owner of the grass-fed dairy where I worked named each cow and talked to them. She had real affection for the cows and explained how they had distinct personalities. Their lives were good, she was fond of saying, with only one bad day.

The thought of consuming protein from happy cows and contented chickens is less guilt provoking than their unfortunate alternative. If the argument is that animals have feelings and feel pain and therefore, we shouldn't eat them, don't delve into plant research too closely. Plants feel pain and even attempt to protect themselves, which explains thorns and noxious sap such as poison ivy.

Researchers at the University of Wisconsin discovered plants, like trees, not only feel pain but warn neighboring plants when danger shows up in the form of plant-eating bug or even fire. Some plants can fold their leaves or release an unpleasant smell, which might discourage a bug, but not fire. Does this make you rethink eating anything ever again?

Then there is the ethics of water usage. Water is a precious commodity and is not to be wasted. An average pound of feed-lot beef takes 1,847 pounds of water to produce a pound of solid protein. Your happy cow who doesn't need tons of water to wash down dry feed only uses 441 pounds of water to produce protein. Compare this to nuts, the go-to protein of non-meat eaters. Almonds are the heavy hitter at 1,929 pounds of water with cashews at 1,704 gallons per pound. No wonder nuts are so expensive.

How should a person handle all this information? Vegetables, fruits, and lentils do use less water. However, most American farmers have chosen to grow feed corn, soybeans, and wheat because of the genetically produced seed of Monsanto that requires almost no effort. We are having a good amount of our produce shipped in, which undoes any water savings because the majority of what is grown in the United States isn't for human consumption because it is mainly feed corn and industrial grade soybeans. Organic farmers make up a small part of the market, but thankfully that share is growing.

How do I handle this ethical dilemma? I continue to eat meat, but less. When I do eat it, I use the grass-fed and pasture-raised versions. Even though some people spend their time thanking God for their food, I prefer to bless or thank the food itself. Each cow, egg, or tomato had a mission to feed someone. The very least I can do is respect that mission and be thankful.

Girl Fights

EVER WONDER WHY SOMETIMES WOMEN and girls have a hard time getting along, especially in larger numbers than two? I was watching an episode of Outlander, a show about a woman thrown back in the more distant past. On the show, the women are working together to dye clothes and having a good time of it. While I realize the show is fiction, women used to get along better than they do today. Why is that?

Comparison and competitiveness, which are pups of the same litter, are the root causes. In earlier times, nothing was easy, and you needed other women to make it through your life. It wasn't unusual to have multiple generations of women living in the same house-hold, and it worked. There was none of this defriending someone or stomping off in a huff because someone said something you didn't agree with. There wasn't the liberty to do so. As a woman, you'd probably end up dying if no one taught you basic life skills. Older women had the responsibility of teaching younger women and children.

With few opportunities for women besides being married, there was always competition. Being a wife and mother was their career. From birth, females were schooled in the need to find a good husband. After marriage, a woman could go back to being friends with her appropriately married friends. If a husband died, the widow became a pariah and a threat to the married women. Mainly, men regarded the widow as an insatiable succubus-type vixen while the women saw her reduced circumstances as something that could happen to them. They stayed away from the new widow, unsure how to handle her and possibly afraid of somehow catching whatever unfortunate circumstance caused her husband to die. Every misfortune was regarded as a divine punishment in the olden times.

Despite the limits and fears, women developed friendships and formed a sisterhood. The more informed women observed that all was not as it should be in the world. To make their voice heard they lobbied for the right to vote. They wanted the right to vote to keep the wrong person out of office and hopefully get a cooler, more intelligent head on the power seat.

Ironically, when our country was founded the idea of women voting was proposed, but individual states voted it down. I imagine the early suffragettes knew about this, and it only spurred on their sense of injustice. Voting banded women together who would not have been friends normally. Rallies were held, awakening hundreds of women to the idea they could want and expect more. To get things back to the way they were, suffragettes were arrested, even though free, peaceful assembly is one of our guaranteed rights. The police were unnecessarily rough, groped, and spat on them. They were kept in jail without food, water, or bathroom privileges while awaiting their husbands or fathers to pick them up. Once they got home, the real beatings started.

About this time, a retired military officer founded the Boy Scouts. He thought boys had forgotten how to be men. The suffragette rallies assured some men that women had forgotten how to be women. A few of those men were publishers and decided what the world needed was more women's magazines. *Ladies Home*

Journal, Better Homes and Gardens, and *Redbook* were born into this climate. The magazines' original intent was not only to give out delicious recipes and show drool-worthy homes but also to keep the lady of the house busy at home and not in the park demanding voting rights. In a sly way, the magazine pitted women against women. Everyone was trying to make their home and garden appear magazine-worthy. It's no telling how many dozens of people were needed even to shoot the magazine spread. One woman could never perform the same magic.

The age of the comparison was in full swing. Along with eyeing your neighbor to see if you were better or worse than the woman next door, a scarcity whispering campaign started. Then again, it's hard to say when the campaign started or if it was always there. Each woman heard she was lucky to have what she had or that no other man would put up with her, even though it may have been the woman putting up with the man. Along with this tidbit came the second boot dropping: other women couldn't be trusted.

At a time, when a man could put his wife aside for burning his dinner or institutionalize her for reading novels, it did sow seeds of distrust. Women went from sisterhood to wary competitors. At that time, it wasn't unusual for men to cheat on their wives. They called it getting their needs met. The double ring wedding didn't become popular until the 1950s. Because most women expected their husband to have a woman on the side, any reasonably attractive woman was a threat. This attitude is carried over into modern life. Why does anyone want a man who cheats?

The seeds of dissension had been sown into the sisterhood. Women, because they were denied so much, guarded what they did have. They assumed, wrongly, that other women were out to steal the things that constituted their life, from their husband to their children.

One of the fallouts from the great magazine manipulation was female self-esteem. Look at an average fashion magazine and you might assume women of the western world are a bunch of emaciated twelve-year-old boys in drag. If you are perusing a lingerie catalog, then it is the same emaciated models only with boob jobs. Even catalogs such as Romans and Lane Bryant tend to use models smaller than the plus sizes they sell.

Advertising is aimed at causing fear in consumers and creating doubt about our self-worth that buying the product will supposedly relieve. Currently, newspapers and magazines are fighting to survive in our digital climate. As the readership in women's magazines declines, perhaps there is hope for increased female self-worth. The UK and Australia have set up specific guidelines to promote no demeaning of genders or generations. Let's hope the United States gets a clue and does likewise.

It's important to remember that despite the abuse, humiliation, and ostracization, Susan B Anthony, Elizabeth Cady Stanton, and other like-minded women endured when they chose not to concentrate on making the best chocolate cake or excel at flower arranging. They persevered and won the right to vote. As women, there is more that unites us than divides us.

If someone implies you fight like a girl, think of it as a compliment because it is, even if they didn't mean it as such!

Voices in the Next Room

IN TAOS, NEW MEXICO, THERE is an odd hum that some say sounds like a diesel engine idling. Others can hear nothing. The noise is referred to as the Taos hum. Scientists have investigated the area numerous times and came up with zip. The most obvious answer is wind, but it happens even when the wind isn't blowing. Some folks were so annoyed by the constant sound, they moved away.

Often, there are sounds some people can hear, but others never do. As a special education teacher, I usually never used fluorescent lights. A flickering one can induce a seizure, and the whine is very distracting, even though most people never notice the high-pitched sound until you mention it.

A small number of people not only hear the whine and hum but also voices. Usually, it is a low murmur, and what is being said isn't distinguishable. This can happen in a quiet room, against the backdrop of white noise such as water running, or even in a noisy room. The usual culprits named are the television or the radio, but often none are playing.

It could be there are actual house sounds the brain tries to make sense of and attach familiar explanations to them. It is rather like the people who see Jesus, Mary, or even Elvis in a piece of burned toast. Their mind tries to make something familiar out of an abstract.

Anyone who watches a sci-fi movie or two knows it is people trapped in another dimension trying to reach us. It might even be ourselves, trying to warn us about the future danger. Possible but not very likely. It could be you're clairaudient. It's a way of having our spiritual ears wide open. A clairaudient person usually talks to themselves. They assume they're providing the answers, but it is more likely a guide.

Clairaudient folks can hear high-pitched sounds that others miss and often find noisy places tiring. Every now and then they could swear their name was called, but there was no one around. The whispering voices could be spirits trying to reach out from the other side.

Residual energy can also contain sound, but because it isn't active energy, the sounds or messages are repetitive. It is also not interactive. Much of the time, a clairaudient can't speak to what they hear, but can only listen. Sometimes, it is like overhearing a conversation. Other times, it is a whispered message across the dimensions meant for the clairaudient person.

Most of the clairs, including clairvoyance, claircognizance–gift of knowing, clairgustance–gift of perception through taste, clairol-factance–spiritual knowledge through smell, and clairsentience, receive information through emotions that are not regarded as real by most folks, which is quite a shame. Consider we are given these skills to navigate our way in this world, but we choose to ignore the road signs.

As for the voices in the next room, do try to listen. They just may have something important to say.

Hexes, Curses, and Blessings

AT A RECENT PSYCHIC WORKSHOP, one participant asked the presenter if she needed to protect herself against someone directing bad energy her way. My ears perked up. I had never worried about this. Maybe I should.

The presenter gave the woman a sympathetic smile. "Do you think you need protection?"

The questioner shrugged her shoulders. "I don't know. There are all these books about psychic protection and everything."

I hadn't read any of those books. Sweet Goddess, maybe I should.

"No worries," the presenter continued. "You only need protection if you think you need protection. Other people aren't hexing you unless you think they are. The power of a curse is your belief in it. If you believe you are cursed, then you are."

It reminded me of the historical romances where the men would never find true love because their ancestor had been cursed centuries ago. Of course, the hero and heroine of the book beat the curse. Did they beat the curse simply because they refused to believe in it?

The presenter went on to say that a person could wear black tourmaline or black obsidian to ward off psychic attack. I penciled that information in my notes as the speaker elaborated.

"The stone is more for your own peace of mind. Your own negative energy could be what is upsetting your life. Without realizing it, you could be cursing yourself and throwing obstacles in your path."

Cursing I knew about. It was so prevalent in our society. Whenever something didn't go exactly as someone wanted, many cursed a blue streak or viewed the results as punishment or a mistake. Very seldom did people stop to analyze the situation for what they could learn from it. Everything happens for a reason. It isn't necessarily a curse or a blessing. All the same, I was aware I had cursed myself for decades.

A simple glance in the mirror could have me groaning. Why wasn't I thinner? Blonde? The list went on forever. I never missed an opportunity to be critical or curse myself. Not too surprisingly, the things I predicted, due to my lack of intelligence, driving ability, etc. usually did happen. Many would call itself a self-fulfilling prophecy. I literally talk myself into situations.

Still, I had to wonder if people could hate you so much, they could hex you? Well, I had my own run-in with a heavy dose of hate and jealousy that did make my life a little difficult. All through high school and afterward I dated the same guy. We had a very good relationship, but I kept breaking up with him. My fear of abandonment never allowed me to fully trust him.

We had great times together and sometimes, we just hung with his buddies. This didn't bother me, and I got to know his friends well. After what I thought was our final breakup, he started seeing a high maintenance chick who was not cool with hanging with his friends or even him seeing his friends. In her neediness, she demanded that all attention be on her. This resulted in a backlash of the friends making a point of telling her they liked me much better than her. Unfortunately, they mentioned me by name.

In our town, no one shared my name, so I was easy enough to

find. Her campaign of hate started, which included hang-up phones calls, nasty notes on my car, and she'd page me at work only to have me go to the lobby to find no one there. The tipping point was she reported my car in a hit and run accident. I must wonder if she deliberately caused the accident.

Since I usually walked to work, the police located my un-scratched car at home with a cold engine, which cleared me of any wrong-doing. It scared me, however, to know the word of an unstable individual could get me in trouble. I decided I had to deal with the issue the only way I knew how. No slap downs, no revenge. Instead, I visited my old boyfriend at his job and explained what was going on. He promised to put a stop to the shenanigans. He ended up breaking up with her, and we started going out again.

As for the girl, what she meant to be a curse for me hurt her. Sure, I was annoyed, but I worked through my problem. Most things are like that. If we believe it's the end of the world, it may feel like it. When I started writing this, I was smack in mercury retrograde, and this time it was meant to impact Pisceans more than any other signs. Being a Piscean, what kind of week did I have?

My husband and I traveled without incident. I received word that my proposal for a workshop was accepted. We dug up a huge crystal point, and I found several other crystals I was looking for. Overall, it was an excellent week full of high points. No complaints. Did it have anything to do with the black tourmaline pendant I usually wear? Good question.

I had read the dire predictions for this week but chose to believe only good would happen. I set my intentions for good things. My lips are just as capable of blessings as curses. Author Ted Andrews reminded me of this by pointing out whenever we see a dead animal on the road that we can bless it and send its spirit on its way.

People used to value blessings much more. I'm old enough to remember loved ones lined up by a dying relative's bed to have a few words with them before they passed on. While some were hoping for whispered information about gold buried in the back yard, most wanted assurance of love and approval—a blessing.

Sons who were about to strike out on their own wanted blessings on their venture, be it college, re-location, or military service. The tradition of asking a father for a daughter's hand was one of soliciting the father's blessing. The blessing was a big deal. Without it, there might have been no marriage or dowry.

Affirmations can be blessings. Verbalizing in the mirror that I like the fact I have two working eyes and strong teeth makes me healthier. I am blessing myself. As for the woman in the class, I have no clue what her situation was. Hopefully, she realizes she's not a victim who is always reacting to things. She can determine her life path. A little black tourmaline, however, never hurts.

Natural Balance

RECENTLY, WE HAVE SQUIRREL AND chipmunk visitors when we have never had them before. I even witnessed a bird and a squirrel eating out of the same feeder. Sometimes, I see mallard ducks eating from the ground beside tiny chickadees. My yard is becoming a sanctuary due to woodlands and former farms being made into expensive neighborhoods with pastoral names such as Whispering Pines or Creekside. Never mind that there are no pines or creeks—and now, no wildlife.

The unfortunate foxes have been sighted and vilified as they try to relocate. One of my neighbors is poisoning all the new visitors. This person is obviously trying to take control of the wildlife in a rather harsh manner. Most people like to quote a verse about having dominion over the animals, which apparently means to kill them. If you look, there are scripture verses about caring for nature and the environment—over one hundred verses. Here's an example. Ezekiel 34:18

> Is it not enough for you to feed on the good pasture, that you must tread down with your feet the rest of your pasture; and to drink of clear water, that you must muddy the rest of the water with your feet?

This verse refers to destroying the environment, which we have done more in the last fifty years than the last fifty-thousand. It doesn't matter if you want to believe in climate change or not. The farmers who sold their land to developers knew they could no longer make a decent living with the unexpected, drastic weather changes. As a person who has been around for over half a century, I have seen the changes.

When I was a child, I remember being out in the fields covered with Monarch butterflies. They were everywhere, sometimes landing on me. Their decline is caused by pesticides, lack of milkweed, which most people cut down, and the weather shift. The warming temperatures cause more hurricanes. Let's face it, butterflies can't fly in a hurricane. It doesn't help that the cave system they used to migrate to is being destroyed, either.

Nature is being wiped out in the name of one species—humans. Back through time, people and animals lived together. Aboriginal populations honored the land. This modern version of man wants to make nature work along their guidelines.

Our bee population is rapidly declining, and the major reason is all the chemicals we put on our lawns. On my daily walk, I see little signs that warn people not to allow children or pets on the lawn for at least a day. If something is bad for humans and pets who are much bigger, it will be even more deadly to insects, bees, butterflies, etc. No bees equal no fruits, no nuts, and most vegetables. Scientists are working on building a mechanical bee as opposed to saving the ones we have.

Bees aren't the only ones in danger. Birds are often the victims of pesticides and herbicides when they eat bugs, seeds, or grain that has been contaminated. At an upscale birdseed store, I overheard a conversation between a shopper and the clerk. The shopper was upset because when she bought suet the birds ate on the side not facing her. The clerk's solution was to leave the suet in its plastic case with the open side facing the window. Did no one consider the birds with their sharp beaks will peck through the plastic and end up ingesting it? This will kill the songbirds the woman was so desirous of seeing. While she may want to feed the birds, she wanted to the birds to operate on her terms.

Plastic is not only a killer for birds but for all marine life, too. It amazes me everything people leave on the beach, a campsite, or even debris that blows off a boat. The manatees spot a plastic grocery bag in the water and assume it is their favorite dinner, jellyfish. Even in waters as far as away as Honduras there are plastic grocery bags in the seagrass. Many countries have dealt with this by not giving you a bag or providing a cheap cloth bag, which I assume people might hold onto as opposed to leaving it on the ground.

As far as nature goes, people assume they are the ultimate authority as what has the right to survive. Wolves were the first to be targeted.

Ranchers often bragged about killing wolves and eventually demanded that Yellowstone Park get rid of the wolves they had due to the disappearance of their cows. Wolves were the answer, but not the correct answer, to their issue since wolves stay away from human inhabitation for good reason. The slight decrease could also be caused by rustlers, lost cows, coyotes, and roaming feral dog packs. Don't overlook some reports of stock loss for insurance purposes, too.

Yellowstone Park complied at the time and relocated the wolves to Canada. The result was the deer took over the park, driving out other wildlife and stripping trees of leaves and bark in their desperate search for food. Yellowstone was no longer a lesson in diversity. As the deer herds grew unchecked, illnesses developed among them. Back in 1995, the wolves were reintroduced into the park. Yes, they did make a dent in the deer population and behavior. Not all the areas were overgrazed, and trees and brush returned, as did the birds.

With the trees came raccoons, possums, and even foxes. Beavers showed up, dammed the river, changing its course. Taking one animal out of the chain not only weakens the chain but can destroy it altogether. Unfortunately, ranchers are once again demanding the wolves be eliminated.

It is rather arrogant, assuming we know what animal is more important. Even now, I must wonder if the remaining wildlife is having a meeting, talking about the troublesome humans who ruin everything.

We fear what we don't know. As a teacher, I see students who stomp on every living creature they see out on the playground, from caterpillars to hurt birds who can't fly. I try to stop them before it is too late. Is this who we have become as a race? We always imagine our enemy is some superior alien race coming to wipe us out. What if we are the enemy? We're killing our own planet and all that lives upon it.

We can all make small adjustments in our daily life to accommodate a better life for every creature on the planet. Use methods that don't involve poison to deter animals you may not want near your home. Herbs such as lemongrass, citronella, basil, and rosemary will discourage mosquitoes. Devices that make sounds too high-pitched for humans to hear will halt rodents from burrowing under your home. Please, pick up your trash. Opt for a stainless-steel travel straw. Carry your own water bottle. Take canvas bags to the store. Use natural pesticides such as neem oil. Planting onions and garlic with your regular plants discourages rodents from nibbling on them. Daffodil bulbs planted with any bulbs rodents like to munch on discourages the behavior. Choose solar or wind power. Trade in your gas guzzler for a more economical vehicle. Walk or bike more.

Spend more time in nature. Realize what a beautiful sight a bumblebee is or even a squirrel eating beside a bird. Take time to sit under a tree or watch a herd of geese lift off. Your world will change for the better when you stop trying to make everything conform to human specifications and accept all life as it is.

Community vs. Individual

MY AUNTS WERE FOND OF talking about how they contributed to WWII. Although neither had skills to work in a factory, the two of them took off to replace the men who had gone to fight. The entire town was filled with women who stepped in when needed. Gardens were planted as food staples became hard to find or non-existent. People often come together as a community during wartime or in a time of shared calamity. At least, they did. My aunts, grandmother, and mother were willing to give up much for the war effort in the hopes of helping the men at the front.

I've lived through the Vietnam War, Bay of Pigs Invasion, Cuban Missile Crisis, the Secret War in Laos, The Invasion of the Dominican Republic, Operation Desert Shield and Storm, Operation Desert Strike, Operation Desert Fox, Operation Infinite Reach, Operation Enduring Freedom, Operation Iraqi Freedom, Operation New Freedom and more. The usual reaction was people were interested at the start if a sacrifice was demanded of them, but often forgot a war was going on if it didn't interrupt their daily life. There was no sense of us in this together. Instead, there was much argument about the politics behind it, but no community. Everyone had their individual opinions about what should be done.

Americans pride themselves on having things their way. Our advertising promises us that things will be made to order, which isn't necessarily true. It leaves people with the idea things should conform to their specifications. Most do not consider the good of the community as they grumble about not having it their way.

In Japan, the community is emphasized to the extreme. Children at the school playground assist any child who falls, brushes off the child, and comforts the child. The teachers don't interfere. By giving the students more responsibility, it helps build a sense of community among them.

Each student is expected to go into a career that will benefit the country. In this regard, students are tested early to see what field they would do well in and are trained for that field. This is much different from the process in America where each student drifts along until they hit high school and are expected to come up with a clue about what they want to do with their lives. The student's decision doesn't take in the welfare of the community. It might be helpful to both the student and the community if it did. They would be plugged into a field where there was a need as opposed to a glut.

Not caring about the community or the future of the community can apply to governments. When dealing with individualistic beliefs, the decisions made aren't the ones that will benefit the community, but rather those making the decision and how they can benefit from it. That's why it is a hard sell to get many elected officials to care about the environment, immigrants, or the poor. Many don't see how these issues will benefit them. A proverb that is often attributed to Wendell Berry is, "We do not inherit our earth, but borrow it from our grandchildren."

Many of those who trumpet individual rights usually mean their rights and for right now. There is no real consideration of the future, even of their own grandchildren. That doesn't mean individuality is wrong. It is more like an idea with potential that became twisted.

The community is everything concept can overwhelm, too.

Cultures that emphasize the community often value conformity. Often, being slightly left of the expected norm can be difficult. Within the community, the square peg child will be expected to fit into a round hole. In Jim Jones's community, his followers were brainwashed into drinking toxic Kool-Aid when investigators arrived. Not all did it. There were a few who didn't buy into the mindset. Nazi Germany could be considered a community that engaged in atrocious activities with the excuse they were under orders, or they didn't know what they were doing. Later stories revealed the German people assumed what they were doing was right because other people were doing it.

It's the classic question. If your friends jump off a bridge, would you do it, too? The question is, is it better to be a community or an individual? We seem to have forgotten how to be a community. People no longer know how to talk to one another. Often, they ignore each other as they stare at their phone and listen to whatever is coming through their earbuds or Bluetooth. When they do react, it's usually with impatience and anger. Someone dared to interrupt their self-absorbed life.

The danger of being a one-hundred-percent community is not living a life true to themselves, or is it? Having taught in Catholic schools, I am very aware of the uniform policy. All the students had matching polos, navy skirts or pants. It was easy for students to resemble each other, but they weren't all the same. Makeup, hairstyle, jewelry, even socks helped the students to create a different look while still similar. When tragedy cut the life of one parochial student short, I saw the community in action. The school was opened on the weekend for the students to gather. Teachers and staff returned without pay to comfort students shocked by death that came unexpectedly to one of their own.

In public schools, when a student dies, how popular he or she was will determine how many students will claim to have known him. An unpopular student will be joked on. An unknown student will pass without comment as if he never existed. A popular student will stop more than a few in their tracks, realizing their own mortality. There will be certain people in the dead students' clique who will experience loss and sadness. Sadly, it will be old news in a couple of weeks. The student's death didn't diminish the community. There wasn't one.

When did we stop caring about our communities, the elderly, or our neighbors for that matter? Some might blame it on air conditioning. We no longer sit on our front porches and visit with our neighbors. Others might blame technology that has us connected to machines and not people. It could be all the extra hours at work that leaves us drained and unwilling to associate with others. Then there is the independence most of us take for granted. We don't need our neighbor's help until we do.

My husband and I were taking advantage of the good weather to do yard work, as were many of our other neighbors, when a scream was heard and someone yelling, "Please help me!" My first reaction was to glance at my husband, who had stopped edging. He had heard it, too. A quick glance at my other neighbors who showed no concern. Farther down our block, a woman was trapped under a car. We rushed to her aid along with a visitor passing by in a car. The rest of our neighbors continued with their lawn mowing and gardening. The woman was rushed to the hospital with broken bones.

The incident made me wonder why so many of the neighbors chose not to react? Perhaps they thought it was none of their business. Maybe they didn't hear because they were plugged into their iPod or phones. It's time for us to rethink the benefits of community and how we can shape one that embraces everyone. Going it alone isn't working. The rise in gun violence can be contributed to additional people having weapons, but it is more about individuals believing others don't have any value to them and are out to get them.

Communities take time and work. It could be as simple as helping someone, smiling, or taking time to listen to a child. Other times, it might involve pooling your resources or even helping someone find their missing pet. In the long run, it is a small price to pay.

The Price of Being Right

EVER MET SOMEONE WHO WAS thoroughly convinced he or she was always right? Never mind anyone else's opinion or input. This same individual assumes everything must be their way because obviously he or she is right. What is the price of being right, even when you are sure you're right beyond a shadow of a doubt?

An intelligent person realizes no one is right all the time. Being right is subjective, too. When taking credit for being right, you are also telling someone else they're wrong. An excellent teacher taught me how to grade essays. She chose to focus on one thing such as grammar or transition sentences when grading an essay as opposed to everything. On the next essay, she would choose another item to critique. Her explanation for her grading system was students could easily be overwhelmed when they saw so many things marked wrong on their paper.

This is also true of adults. As a teacher, I would get a yearly, sometimes twice a year, evaluation from the principal. Good administrators made a point of telling me things I did right as opposed to picking apart my lesson plan. Truthfully, most of whatever the principal would say would merely be his opinion or preferences, not necessarily the right way for me to teach.

When we decide we are right and must share this information at all costs, it says much more about us than we might like. As both a parent and teacher, I listened to numerous anecdotes from children without correcting them when they got a word wrong or even a misidentified a place. Their tales weren't tests, but a natural desire to share.

Ever been miffed when describing a movie, a book, or even a vacation you went on, only to have another person correct you? As well as you can remember, he or she didn't go on vacation with you. It also ruins your flow of conversation and bleeds away some of your joy.

Sure, there's a specific date when a state joined the union, but most declarations of rightness are merely opinions. Sometimes, they can be the result of misinformation and other times the belief someone has in him or herself that they are an expert on everything.

Often silence when someone is holding forth on a subject is considered confirmation. Most decide it isn't worth the hurt or angry feelings to correct or contradict. They decided maintaining a work relation or a friendship was more important. Real friendships can withstand disagreements or preferring different things. It isn't a matter of right or wrong. Black and white thinkers want to label things right and wrong. What's up with that?

When another person disagrees with their beliefs, or opinions, it may make them feel threatened, which could explain why they have the need to be overly assertive. They unroll their beliefs like a standard and declare them as a truth, then are appalled when someone comments on it. When I was younger, all controversial subjects such as politics, religion, and sex were kept private. There were certainly fewer people trumpeting their views.

Once when I attended church with my grandmother, I heard a lady make a historically inaccurate statement that I wanted to correct. Grandmother must have known my intention because she gave my hand a squeeze and shook her head. Later, on the way home, she explained that my eager correction would have embarrassed the woman. In the end, demonstrating my recently acquired knowledge would not have won me any prizes or gained praise. Just the reverse, I would have marred the elderly woman's day and earned myself the derogatory name of smart mouth.

Our culture has changed with celebrities holding forth on every subject as self-declared experts. It's not surprising Joe or Jane Average want their moment in the limelight, pontificating on what they know or think they know. Having a rigid need to be right tends to drive people away, muttering complaints about difficult to work with or even more unflattering descriptions.

In the end, those who insist they're right at every opportunity, often drive away friends, relatives, and sometimes significant others. It is a high price to pay for a dubious honor.

Animals as Messengers

THE MORNING RADIO NEWS REPORTED that a new study reveals in tough emotional situations people generally talk to their dogs—not to other people. An article by Hal Herzog entitled *Why People Care about Animals More Than Other Humans,* illustrated that women felt their pet provided more emotional support than their family did. The article went on to point out that people are more outraged over an animal being shot by the police than a human. This speaks a great deal as to how we feel about animals.

Most people like animals, even to the point of trying to interact with them. This is evidenced by people wanting to pet dogs, feeding birds, and taking countless wildlife photos. Did you ever consider animals want to communicate with us? That they even have messages for us? The two most obvious questions are what is the message and how do you know a blue jay just didn't stop by for breakfast as opposed to delivering a message.

Ancient cultures and even aboriginal cultures today believe in the power of animal messages. There is no clear view of who is the ultimate source behind the animal messengers. Many consider it is the animal itself that is also a part of the universal tapestry. Others credit the collective consciousness, fairies, nature spirits, and ancestors. In the end, there is a message being sent special delivery to you.

Any animal you noticed that is out of place for your area, that acts out of character, or even keeps reoccurring can be your animal messenger. One that kept showing everywhere for me was a red-winged blackbird. There had never been any in our area before. It sat on the eave of a house when I walked my dog. It appeared on a street sign when I went to the grocery, and I saw it again on my way back from the grocery on the same street sign. Many people passed by this same bird but didn't see it. My attention was drawn to it because it had a message for me.

When you glimpse an animal, you think could be your messenger, try to remember what issue had been troubling you. It could also be a plan you might be considering. Then look up the animal symbolism. There will be plenty of sites to choose from online or you can pick up *Communicating with Animal Messengers* or a pocket guide by Ted Andrews or Dr. Steven Farmer. If you're online, there will be tons of things about your animal messenger. It's up to you and your intuition to determine which one fits.

On the morning of my workshop, I spotted a trio of hawks circling as I hiked through an unfamiliar woods. At one point, I became lost but noticed the hawks were still with me. I remembered birds of prey from their high position in the sky remind us to look at the big picture. I followed the birds back to the road that led back to camp. As I neared the camp, a robin flew ahead and landed in front of me and sang. Another messenger, the robin represents the throat chakra, happiness, contentment, renewal, and new beginnings.

You can have more than one animal messenger per day. I obviously needed to be reminded to look at the big picture. It was only one workshop, and I had presented it many times before. The robin's song encouraged me to speak my truth. My early morning walk and meeting my messengers eased my anxiety.

Every animal you spot will not be an animal messenger. Some-times, animals come to you in your dreams. Mythological, exotic, and extinct animals often meander through our dreams since they can't in our real lives. Yes, you can look up these animals in various manuals. Every now and then, you'll come across a creature no one chose to write about or very little is written about it.

In that case, research the animal. Find out on your own about its habitat and life. By doing so, you'll discover your message while learning a little more about the natural world. Animals play such a vital part in our physical and spiritual world.

While many people have spirit guides who have the appearance of a person, others prefer animal spirit guides. Especially children who have been abused by adults can find comfort in an animal spirit guide.

There may be animals that show up quite a bit in your life, dreams, or you find yourself drawn to their image. These are sometimes referred to as your totem animals. When you need certain characteristics to power through a problem, the creature who has those traits makes an appearance in your life. Totem animals can exchange places as your life changes, too. My go-to totem animal used to be a bear. It represents both healing and teaching. For the most part, a bear pursues its life at a leisurely pace and with all feet on the ground.

An owl appeared in my life, from roosting in one of the nearby trees to showing up in meditations and dreams. It didn't mean the bear had left, but I was now at a point in my life that I needed the owl energy.

The secret to meeting your animal messengers is simply to be aware and take opportunities to be outside more. It can be as a walk outside on your lunch hour, drinking your morning beverage on your porch, or making a trek to a nearby woods or park. Start journaling about your dreams. It might surprise you to find an animal has been making regular appearances in your dream world. There are several spirit animal meditations on YouTube you can try.

Remember animal messengers want to help and encourage. They would never deliver a message of doom and gloom. So, if you get a negative message, realize it is a matter of interpretation.

The Fairies Are Among Us

LAST YEAR A PROTECTIVE SYMBOL appeared in my back yard and wasn't put there by human hands. It was a large triangle pointed toward my house in parallel lines of mixed stones. Ninety-six to be exact. Some were river rocks, one was a white rock shaped liked a femur bone, a few were ruby zoisite, which is the stone of patience and transforming negative energy into positive. The beautiful polished stone originates from Tanzania, which is far, far away. The zoisite is also a calming stone, which I may have needed because my new neighbors and their aggressive canines were ruining my back yard for me.

When we moved in seven years ago, I liked the couple who lived behind us. They were a good-natured couple with a friendly golden retriever who would often visit whenever a cookout took place. Ray, the elderly golden, would calmly approach whoever was grilling and take a seat near them. He usually was rewarded with a burnt hot dog for his good manners. They moved and were replaced by neighbors with extremely vicious dogs.

Animals are my thing, but these dogs were far from friendly. One appeared in my side yard and tried to attack me. My neighbors finally got a fence they attached to our own, but that did little to calm down the hounds. They were outside all the time and constantly barking at me or any family member that dared to come out. Whenever my aged pooch came outside, they went crazy. Somehow, they bit one of the other neighbor's Yorkies through the fence, putting permanent punctures in the tiny dog's ears. No one was a fan of these dogs.

The yard had been my natural sanctuary. After long winter months, there was nothing I liked better than tilling the soil and planting seeds. My husband and I used to sit in our lawn chairs and watch the birds at the feeders. Even the birds were disturbed by the dogs' constant barking and hurling themselves against the fence. The fence panel came loose after one of the crazed dogs consistently hurled itself against it. I found myself inches away from the dog's snapping snout.

In retrospect, I'd like to pretend I handled the moment in a mature, serene matter. I did not. A series of curse words flew from my mouth, some directed at the snapping dog as I pushed the sagging fence in place. Then I screamed for my husband to bring the hammer and nails. We hammered the fence back in place but couldn't do the same for the serenity that had been ripped from my back yard natural sanctuary.

It was a summer without fire pits because we could barely hear ourselves talk with the dogs constantly baying, howling, and throwing themselves against the fence. The neighbor whose dog was bitten moved. The neighbor on the other side of me moved, too. It was as if they couldn't wait to get away—a feeling I understood. My husband did his best to serve as a buffer between the neighbor and me by asking the neighbor not to spray his toxic chemicals near the fence line since I had wildflowers growing on the other side.

Retreat was my only option. Instead of enjoying the summer in my yard, I watched the birds from inside the house and at the occasional park. During this time, I asked the fairies to help me. Not with the dogs. I hadn't thought of that, but with the various plants and wildlife that took shelter in our yard.

While waiting for a time when I could use the yard for myself and for rituals, I put out gnome statues to attract gnomes. I also scattered quartz crystal in the flower gardens, hoping to attract the fairies. Fairy is a general name that covers over two hundred different entities. My goal was to bring out the gnomes. Traditionally, gnomes are caretakers of the garden. They are believed to protect minerals or buried treasure. They will often draw crystals into the ground since they love them so much. Some beliefs center on gnomes being both good luck and guardians. This is why the statues are placed in gardens, houses, even barns.

The day I discovered the stones I was cutting grass. I may have discovered the femur stone first since it was white and stood out against the grass. Afraid I might run over them with a lawnmower, I picked up a couple of stones and put them in a bucket. There were dozens of stones all in a pattern in the tall spring grass. I took a photo of them, then picked them up. When my husband arrived home, I asked him if this was an elaborate trick of his, although it was not like this behavior was part of his nature.

He hadn't done it. We have a six-foot privacy fence and the gate is locked from the inside. There was no rational explanation. After we threw out normal possibilities, we had to accept it was a mystical occurrence, and my husband urged me to put out the rocks as I found them. I did.

Since I did not consider myself an expert on natural phenomenon, I carried my photo around and asked those with more expertise to examine it. Powerful, protective magic one described it. Another told me I had fairies in the yard, most likely gnomes since the stones had been selected and pushed up through the ground as opposed to being laid on the grass. At a crystal workshop, the instructor laid out a similar stone grid to provide psychic protection. The grid in the back yard was for me, my household, and all who were in the yard.

Strange things started happening. The neighbors with the obnoxious dogs often called in their dogs whenever they spotted me in the yard filling up the bird feeders. They also put up a barrier around their back porch where I couldn't see them. Their attitude struck me as fearful as they all scurried into the house whenever they saw me. It was that crazy woman who sings to the flowers and ties ribbons to the trees. They were ribbons with intentions. I didn't care what the neighbors said. What I wanted were things to go back to the way they were.

One day on my walk through the neighborhood, I noticed my annoying neighbor had put up a for sale sign. The next day their house sold, causing me to wonder if they had underpriced it. A week later they were gone, as were their dogs. The new neighbors were a friendly couple with an elderly dog.

Odd that the neighbors would move, especially since the wife told me this was their last home, and there would be no more moving for her. Since a year had come and gone, it was spring again. This time when my husband went to mow, all the stones were missing, possibly because they'd accomplished what they were supposed to do.

Yes, the neighbor with the out-of-control hounds did move, but it was more than that. The gnomes wanted me to know they were there and showed me in a very real way. They also taught me the importance of patience. Now it is time to select the perfect thank you gift. I'm thinking crystals with a scattering of silver coins.

Throwaway People

A FRIEND RECENTLY CONFIDED NOW that she had reached the other side of fifty and put on some weight, she often found herself ignored by the general public. It was like she was invisible. Before, when she was younger and thinner, at least the men paid attention to her. Often, she'd received negative attention from women due to her curvaceous physique in her younger years. Now she could walk through a crowded room, leave through another door, and no one would even notice.

Malcolm Gladwell, in his book, *Blink,* explains the phenomenon where we sum up in a matter of seconds if a person is a danger, a possibility, or useless. The viewer who makes the snap judgment is trying to decide how a person might fit into their lives for good or bad. My friend has slipped into the useless category and has become invisible for practical purposes.

In a few seconds, a person decides if a person could be a possible romantic partner, friend, useful as far of obtaining financial or career goals, a threat, or having no useful purpose in regards to the viewer. A person is dismissed or labeled in under ten seconds. For all basic purposes, the person was mentally thrown away.

There are so many people in our society that are considered throwaway people. Homeless, elderly, and prisoners possibly vie for first billing. Somewhere along the line, people gave up all these folks. An employer, family, or clergy made the decision it would be better to not have this person in their lives. Advertising and social media exclude them. Big cities even round up the homeless before big events to tidy up their town.

Crimes against the homeless, the criminal element, hookers, and the poor are the least likely to be solved. Those who commit crimes against this population aren't master criminals, but they are smart enough to realize that law enforcement will be directed toward more influential victims. However, those who are part of this lower echelon are entrenched in the don't squeal culture where clue tips aren't forthcoming.

Being apathetic toward someone can be like a fast-moving virus in some regards. When I traveled to various schools to work with special education students, I noticed there was a pecking order. The child who was shunned by his peers, I made into my assistant for the day. This wasn't always easy because there was usually a reason the child had been ostracized. By the end of the day, the other children were interested in the child. Curious as to what I saw in the formerly ignored student, the other students would engage him in conversation or even invite him to play. If I was at a school for a long assignment, I could nurture that student until he or she was able to adequately engage with his peers. Often, my assignments were short and when I returned the student was once again ignored. Surprisingly, teachers engaged in ignoring the forgotten students. Maybe it was an oversight, but it still happened.

In Educational Psychology, we were shown a film called *The Story of a Cypher*. A cypher can sometimes be defined as an empty set for mathematical purposes. The short movie was about a teen boy who died and a teacher who was asked to write his obituary. No one knew much about the student. He wasn't brilliant or a problem student, either. The teacher went on a research mission and discovered the boy had entered first grade with an upbeat attitude and an artistic bent. With the death of his father, he fell behind the other students, never to catch up. Instead of a glowing report like his initial ones, there were summaries concluding not much could be expected from the boy. How incredibly sad that people gave up on him so early.

The special needs population is another forgotten group or at best avoided. Most people feel uncomfortable around them because they're unsure how to respond. A dear friend was in an accident that forced her into a wheelchair. She often complained that people worked hard not to *see* her. I often held the heavy entry doors open for her since they were not automatic. Few did. I'm not sure why. Perhaps, they were afraid of an awkward conversation if she insisted, she was *handi-capable*.

Every one of these throwaway people has so much to teach us. According to the book, *Embraced by the Light*, those who appear to be disadvantaged may be on a higher soul level. They chose a harder path.

Everyone is deserving of dignity and respect. From my Down syndrome students, I learned to celebrate the smallest thing from the sunshine to a smile. Female inmates taught me the difference between me and them was one bad decision and the importance of being called by their first name. Those in nursing homes are full of wisdom and historical anecdotes for those who will listen. Instead of being someone tied into a wheelchair, they can recall participating in the Civil Rights Marches.

As a people watcher, I witness people rushing around in a frenzy, not even bothering to say excuse me to the person they've bumped into. It's sad we are in such a hurry we don't have time for civility. Even worse is when we label others as non-useful or to be avoided.

Balance

IN THE MORNINGS, I CREEP outside and enjoy my tea with the sunrise as I watch the birds at the feeders. Usually, one bird alights on the feeder, the next bird perches directly opposite of it. This goes on until the entire ring is filling with hungry birds. Occasionally, a bird might land not on the right spot, causing the feeder to rock madly and the other birds to fuss in protest until the bird flies away or moves to the right spot. When a big bird arrives, they depart, leaving the big bird to manage the feeder balancing act on its own. The bird usually drops immediately to the ground to eat. What I learned from my early morning observations is birds understand balance. As do the squirrels who run along the top of my fence. The creatures who don't are people.

We have difficulties finding balance in many areas of our lives. Driven individuals are all about work neglecting themselves and their families in the pursuit of a career. Others might be caught up in appearances and seeing the gym manager more than they do their friends. Still others take no time to reflect on their lives. This lack of reflection causes imbalance.

Industrialized nations, except for the United States, are providing more vacation and comp days for their workforce. They've understood that the human spirit, body, and mind needs downtime to recharge. Progressive companies such as Google provide napping tents and onsite daycare aware that rested and happy employees perform better.

Most people would relish a few days off. Four-day weekends delight most folks, but probably not the workaholics. When we have time to rest and create, we are more content. Instead, of dividing our days into neat little thirds, we instead run full blast in one area with promises that we will make it up later, which we never do.

We keep going until we fall ill or die. In the film, *Happy*, we meet the widow of a man who literally worked himself to death. Sometimes unsuspected influences throw us out of whack. Blaine Schmaltz, a North Dakota farmer, always felt ill after spraying his fields with pesticide. One day he passed out in the field and was diagnosed with having occupational asthma. After suffering from various illnesses, he decided to change to organic farming. He not only worried about what the chemicals were doing to him, but to his family and land, too. After working chemical-free, he felt better, and as time progressed, his medical issues vanished, too.

Blaine's body was out of balance. Once he learned what to do to correct the issues, his health returned. When we shoulder too much responsibility or internalize conflict, anxiety or fear it often comes out in physical symptoms such as ulcers or tension headaches. On-going stress can even present itself in chronic diseases.

There are several ways to deal with stress, anxiety, or even de-pression. It isn't watching television or scrolling through social media. Doctors are prescribing time in nature for everything from anxiety to attention deficit disorder. Not too surprising since nature is our original environment, not climate-controlled boxes devoid of sunlight. A simple walk through a park can boost our energy and creativity levels.

Breathing, techniques, meditation, even journaling help alleviate stress. Yoga stretches before bed will ease the transition into a restful slumber. Quiet time, which can be anything from walking, coloring, or simply reflecting on the day, allows the body and mind a break. Gratitude, the act of counting your blessings, not only makes people less anxious but more content.

When you feel overwhelmed, as many often do, take time to analyze what is going on in your life. Are you trying to do too much? If you're saying no one else will do it if I don't, then it could be an activity that needs to be discarded because no one cares enough to continue it. The world won't come to an end if you do.

Like the farmer who was being poisoned by his use of pesticide, perhaps you, too, are being exposed to toxins. Examine what you are eating, chemicals in your home, yard, and toiletries. There are many organic alternatives to choose from. There are plenty of recipes online for DIY organic cleaning supplies and toiletries.

People, media, and work environments can be mentally draining. Everyone knows a friend, relative, or co-worker who can suck all the energy out of a room with their attitude. Face it, you will not change these people, but you can set boundaries to protect yourself. No one ever said they felt better checking their social media several times a day. Social media has been linked to poor sleep habits, hyperactivity, and depression. It's hard to feel good about your life when everybody and their brother is bragging about their exotic vacation and posting drool-worthy photos.

According to *The Beauty Myth*, women's attitudes improved about themselves when they didn't read fashion magazines, watch commercials or were exposed to unrealistic body images. Know what your triggers are and limit your contact to them. It will help.

Before you finish reading this, take time to see if you take time to play, laugh, and enjoy the moment. Be aware of the good in your life. It is okay to sit in nature and listen. You might be surprised by what you hear and learn. Write down your activities for a week and see what area is missing out on time. It probably isn't work. Adjust your schedule and don't be apologetic about it, either. You'll be surprised how much happier you and your family will be.

Ridicule

AS A TEEN, THE POLISH jokes were popular jokes and always ended with the punch line that's pretty good for a Pollock. The inference was Poles were stupid. At the time, *Saturday Night Live* was running skits about Eastern European males who were clueless about the American culture. Even though I participated in the jokes, I did consider them mean-spirited. The excuse I gave myself was I didn't know anyone who was Polish.

With a good chance there were other students of Polish descent in that atmosphere, they'd never admit it, especially when the term Pole was associated with idiot. Fortune has allowed me to travel, and I've discovered in various countries there is always one group, maybe more, that is disrespected. The victims of the jokes are usually poor, powerless, and unable to retaliate in any meaningful way. It's the same as kicking a blind and toothless dog. How did the topic of the jokes respond?

A friend explained to me that there was a prayer going around for women of color that started, *Goddess, grant me the confidence of a mediocre white male.* The simple sentence is loaded. It basically says that white men assume the world is theirs for the taking. The fact the women need this prayer shows the world is not theirs for the taking. My ex-husband, who was a Southerner, told me the poor whites took pride in not being black. It seems an odd thing to take pride in since you have no control over your birth.

On the other hand, if you chose, via reincarnation, to be born into the family you were born into, there is a purpose behind it. No one should pity you or ridicule you for your ethnic group, economic status, intellectual capacity, faith, or lack of one. This disrespect is, at best, childish behavior. With time, most of us grow out of it. Unfortunately, if we spend our time around disrespectful folks, we go right back to the junior high behavior.

In a recent episode of the *On Being* radio show, individuals decided to start dialogues with people of differing opinions. One was a Harvard professor who had been raised by a teen mother on welfare. He spoke to a man who was against all forms of public assistance and had never met a person who had benefitted from the system. Name-calling and finger-pointing are easy when you never meet the object of your scorn.

Eleanor Roosevelt is known for saying "Do the thing you fear."

Most of us react out of fear whether we recognize it or not. Currently, many people huddle behind gated communities, afraid of their fellow humans and elect officials who promote divisive politics.

My grandmother told us how she crossed the street whenever she saw a Catholic church or a Knights of Columbus Hall. Her father told her to do so, convinced they would harm Protestant children. Since there wasn't a giant purple P on her forehead, I'm not sure how they would know what religion she was.

Along with fear, comes ignorance as barriers to acceptance of our fellow person. Then there are the people who take a tidbit of information they know or may have heard and apply it to the entire group. When I met my ex-sister-in-law, she informed me she knew all about Hoosiers because she worked with one. She went on to add, we only ate the legs off a turkey, not the entire bird. I told her that wasn't true, and I didn't even like turkey legs. You can't judge the residents of a state by one person. Because she only knew one person, she assumed it was true for all.

If you know no one, then you are fed all sorts of stereotypes by the media and associates. It's hard to care about a one-dimensional character of a group while it isn't uncommon for people to seek out stories to support their belief. Never mind that they are based on ignorance.

Getting back to the Harvard professor, when he was able to sit down and talk to someone who thought welfare should be abolished, it started a dialogue. Do likewise. Start a dialogue with people who aren't like you. As for other religions, find out more about them. In my children's confirmation class, they traveled to places of worship of different faiths. The point was to know and respect different religions. The pilgrims came to America to have religious freedom. Now there is a movement afoot to put down religions that do not conform with the majority.

The great thing about respecting others is that respect is usually returned to you. If you choose to treat someone with respect, it doesn't mean you share their beliefs, but accept that they do have them. My husband isn't a big believer of gnomes in our back yard, but he accepts that I am. Part of this acceptance is not ridiculing another's belief.

When we go to visit conservative relatives, we may buy them books they want that support their belief system and allow them to pray in front of us and sometimes over us. This is their belief system. Our job isn't to convert them to our way of thinking.

People who declare themselves agnostic or atheist are just as deserving of acceptance. In a polarized climate, they have taken up the much heavier burden. Every day, they are confronted with bumper stickers, banners, billboards, not to mention people, who tell them they are going to Hell or are dammed, or are horrible people, in general.

If people did apply the Golden Rule, by treating people the way they wanted to be treated, the world would be a much more peaceful and happier place. As for jokes, anything that ridicules someone else isn't humorous, at all. Thankfully, I have given up jokes at the expense of others.

Meaningful

IT'S HARD TO GO ANYWHERE without being told to live in the now or to do something meaningfully. My recent online food diary explained to me I needed to be eating meaningfully. This puzzled me for a while until it was explained. Most in the western world tend to eat while watching television, which explains why there is almost always a television in most restaurants and bars. It's hard to get anyone under thirty to consume food without a cellphone in the opposite hand. Don't forget the working lunch, which is a good way to spoil a meal.

The point of eating meaningfully was to be aware of what is consumed. By being focused on other things, a person is unaware of how much they've eaten. It explains putting away a huge bucket of popcorn in a darkened movie theatre. By having our attention on other things, we fail to notice the flavors and textures of the food. We also miss out on signals that our body may be sending saying we are full.

Those who don't eat mindfully will eat bad food without realizing it immediately. To lose weight, I decided to eat at the table, arrange my food in a becoming manner on the plate, and to eat slowly and appreciate each bite. Sometimes, I even thanked the food for its job in providing nutrients.

The weight did come off as I took time to enjoy each bite. Since my attention was on my food and not the television, I stopped eating sooner. It made me consider what other things I should do mean-ingfully. As an organized person, I always had lists of things to do. Often, it felt like my life consisted of surviving one event, then on to the next. The sad part was I didn't relish meals I'd labored over. Instead, I made sure everyone had plenty, then it was on to the dishes.

Each year was a chain of events for me to juggle along with work and home duties. There were scouts, sports, school events, birthdays, holidays, and vacations. All I remember was rushing around to get things done. There are very few moments when I sat down and was in the moment. Unlike my children, I didn't have funny stories to tell about a holiday. All I had were regrets about how I should have done something differently or fixed an additional dish. There was little pleasure in the memories.

When was the last time I did something where I wasn't multi-tasking? As a mother, I was always doing two to three things at once. According to *Psychology Today* magazine, when you multi-task you don't do any of the tasks well and your memory of doing them can be quite iffy. It might explain why most of the events passed by me in a blur.

The article made me stop and think about how I rush through life and on to the next task, which is no more pressing or important than the previous one.

Doing something meaningfully is not doing a mediocre job. In organic gardening, I learned that plants have a mission. It could be to produce fruit or flowers. Everything within the plant is directed toward the mission. The plant gives it all in a variety of circumstanc-es. Never once did I hear a plant say it wasn't going to be a plant today. Nor did it try to produce fruit while comparing itself to another plant and becoming disheartened about all that it wasn't. My Druidic friend reminds me to thank the plants every time I pick a flower or pluck an apple from the tree. Gratitude is called for when someone, or in this case some plant, has given its all.

Doing things in a meaningful manner is not new. In fact, it is very retro. In ancient times, people were expected to do their best. To do so, you must pay attention to your work, and be in the moment. If you're present in your work, then you'll also be present in your leisure.

I've been taking my morning tea outside and enjoying the birds while they eat. It's only if it takes to drink a cup of tea. That's all I do is watch the birds and enjoy my tea, but I am there for every second. Not too surprisingly, it is one of the things I do remember about my day.

Next time you hear someone say something about doing something in a meaningful way, consider if there is anything you could apply it to.

Rituals Matter

AS A CURIOUS PERSON, I want explanations and love to explore new to me cultural experiences and religions. A Hindu friend of ours offered to take us to the local temple of a differing religion. It was very popular and thousands visited weekly. Normally, my husband and I stick out in India with our height, light skin, and his blonde hair. This time was no different. Following the posted rules, we donned headdresses, checked our shoes and observed a respectful silence. We followed the rules as much as we could and there were many rules.

All the same, our Hindu friends were chided for several infractions from answering a cell phone to carrying shoes as opposed to depositing them at the shoe check. At the museum, I received a free booklet about the religion that announced they were not a slave to rituals. About the same thing Martin Luther said when he nailed his grievances against the Catholic church to the cathedral door. It's popular to be against rituals, but rituals help and connect us.

Take, for example, that getting ready for bed rituals inform our body and mind that we are getting ready to relax. It may take the form of a hot bath, a cup of herbal tea, or shutting down the electronics or lights. Anyone who has gone to bed at a late hour with the hopes of falling asleep immediately realizes how hard this is to do without an associated ritual.

Social rituals, such as family dinners, often bring feelings with them that deepen over time. (It's the type of thing that you don't appreciate until it is no longer happening.) Everyday activities can be rituals based on the steps and repetition and how we think of them.

Friday is movie night for my husband and myself. We either rent a movie or watch one on television. This signals the end of the work week and allows us to have quality time. We almost always have pizza, which is part of our routine. Even when traveling, we try to continue our ritual because it gives us a sense of continuity.

Weddings, birth celebrations, and deaths have rituals. They mark shifts into different life stages. Without ritual, changes are a little more difficult to maneuver. Is it the ritual itself or how we feel about it that makes things a little easier? According to a *Scientific American* article entitled "Why Rituals Work," it could be a little bit of both. Rituals even work for people who don't believe they work.

An experiment was done with volunteers that had a lottery of two hundred dollars that only one volunteer could win. Each volunteer wrote about and discussed what they would do with the money. Then the winner was announced. Those who didn't win were divided into two groups. One wrote about their unhappiness in not winning, while the others did the same, but their ritual included sprinkling salt on the paper, tearing it up, then counting. Those who did the second procedure were less angry and able to move on.

Sometimes, not connecting with rituals doesn't allow us to go to the next stage in life. Case in point, social media has decimated many of our rituals associated with ending relationships. Not only can a person end a relationship with a text, but they can stalk their ex endlessly on social media, never ever breaking the connection. Gone is the cryfest, returning each other's gifts, or the ceremonial burning of shared photos. While this may have seemed over the top to some, it served a purpose of a physical and emotional closure. Instead, we have turned into a nation of voyeurs who are concerned with the lives of past partners to such an extent that there isn't time or energy left to create new relationships.

We all have rituals, although sometimes we call them habits. Every morning, I get up, greet the dog, prepare lunches and fill the tea kettle. I let the dog out and watch him while I listen for the tea kettle. This is part of my morning ritual. Any disruption to this ritual doesn't ruin my day, but leaves me feeling vaguely unsettled as if I left a door open somewhere. Rituals matter. Don't believe me, delve into the life of any professional athlete.

Michael Jordan admits when he played for the Chicago Bulls, he wore his college basketball shorts under his regular uniform. Many sports legends have pre-game rituals from eating certain foods before a game to even wearing lucky underwear. From actors to gamblers, they all have their rituals. The power is in the belief. Some people are doing rituals to ward off bad luck while others invite in good luck.

Not too surprisingly, doing shared rituals in a group can be even more effective. Some might say it helps to be surrounded by those who have similar beliefs. It could be the power of conscious thought, too. Shamanic healing is very ritualistic, but many have admitted to feeling increased power or health when more than one shaman was attending. Was it the combined power of the two healers or the belief that two healers were better than one?

Recently, it's been an accepted practice to ridicule those who engage in ritualistic behavior for whatever reason. If you have a co-worker who takes a break at a certain time, uses the same coffee cup, and sits in the exact same chair in the lounge, there might be the temptation to refer to her as being OCD (obsessive compulsive disorder), when in truth, she has found a ritual that works for her.

Shared rituals build a sense of community. This explains why people who may no longer believe in a certain religion will still attend services. An atheist shared via a blog that it was lonely being an atheist since there were no services on Sunday or any other day he could attend and share that sense of being part of a shared group.

As a young parent who was raising three kids alone, I discovered the excitement of Christmas lasted for about the twelve minutes it took to rip open the presents after months of waiting. I needed a break from being the sole entertainer and decided to take the kids to the movies. Part of their holiday ritual was deciding which movie they would see. Even though the kids have all moved out, they often join me at the cinemas on Christmas day for our own family holiday ritual.

If a ritual is abhorrent to you, such as one that demeans or belittles you, then it shouldn't be part of your life. As the architect of your life, you get to decide what rituals stay or go. You also can create your own family rituals, too. No reason to hold onto the ones that never worked for you.

As for the temple we attended that didn't believe in rituals—they had a ton of them.

Walking

RUNNERS EXIST IN THEIR OWN world where their daily schedule focuses around when they can get their distance work in, along with interval training, and cross training. They prefer to hang out with other runners who are more than willing to discuss upcoming road races, the benefits of carb loading, and the newest running gadgets to hit the market. Sometimes, a runner may even dash into traffic without waiting for a light because they're in the cardiac zone. More likely, they have headphones on and are unaware of what's happening on the road beside them. The hardest thing for a runner to understand is someone who can run, but doesn't. (This is true of members of various segments of society.)

Such was the case with my ex-husband, a hard-core runner. He assumed because I ran in high school and had long legs that I had to run. (There was no Title IX at that time and running was one of the few sports open to women, possibly because there wasn't much expense involved since they had already built a track for male runners.)

For a time, I ran to be one of those running couples. Even though I could go the distance, I had no desire to run until I felt like I would throw up. Instead, I wanted to stroll leisurely along enjoying the breeze, the bird song, and flowers. On occasion, I would even wave or stop to talk to a neighbor. According to Dr. Oz, walking is the perfect exercise for almost everyone, especially middle-aged females.

About the only time I might break into a run is when the airport announces that boarding is ending for my intended flight. This lack of desire to run wasn't something my ex-husband could understand. You might say he never walked a mile in my shoes. On one hand, I had the option of running, which I did for several years before I decided I never liked it and simply stopped.

How often do we do things simply because it is trendy, to satisfy someone else's need for us to do so, or even because we are told to do it? People make assumptions without taking in the big picture, and considering options, too.

After our second business trip to India, I became upset with an American journalist who insisted Indians had a death wish because of their driving and tendency to ride two to three to a scooter and sometimes squeezing an entire family on one small two-wheeled vehicle. The journalist went on to point out that they didn't have car seats for their children, which meant they didn't care. Perhaps they were ready to die because they would just be reincarnated again. (I will have to admit I immediately stopped reading anything by this journalist because that one statement contained both arrogance and ignorance.) This is often the case when we see everything through our view point only, which goes back to walking a mile in someone else's shoes.

Having been in Delhi rush hour traffic, I noticed no one drives that fast ever and there is an amazing lack of accidents because people are focused on their driving and honor the folks on the bike rickshaws as much as the buses. They also allow the pedestrians to cross along with the cows. It was hard for me to get used to the idea that if I walked in traffic people would stop. They did, but I usually chose to walk with a crowd as not to test it too much.

The mentioned journalist blithely assumed everyone in India believed in reincarnation and had a death wish. There are many religions in India and not all believe in reincarnation. As for car seats, it's not going to work on a scooter. Who am I to say there aren't car seats in some of the cars?

As baby boomers, my husband and I can remember standing up in a moving car, crawling over the seats while the car was in motion, and even riding in the driver's lap, supposedly helping to drive. While seatbelts were invented in 1959, most car owners considered them a nuisance and cut them out. Public safety campaigns alerted the car owners to the importance of wearing a seatbelt with limited success in the United States. In 1989, a law was passed that made it mandatory to wear seatbelts in the back and front seats. Still, you could not be pulled over for not wearing a seatbelt, but you could be cited if you were pulled over for something else. With the invention of traffic cams, you could be photographed and have the ticket mailed to you. Not too surprisingly, this increased the use of safety-belts.

We didn't wear seatbelts because we didn't believe in reincarnation, but rather because we didn't want a pricey ticket. According to data provided by the National Safety Council, the safest time to drive was in the early 1940s, when most of the young men were overseas at war. Traffic fatalities have taken a huge jump in recent years due to driving while tired, drunk and distracted due to cell phone usage. Then, there is the road rage battles that often take place on the highway. It begs the question of which nation's inhabitants might have a death wish.

When we assume someone could do something safer or better,

we naturally assume they have the same options as we do. Why doesn't that woman leave her abusive spouse? Could be she feels she has no skills or support team that would allow her to make it on her own. Could be she is brainwashed into believing that her life is as good as it gets. There may be no domestic abuse shelters in her area or it's against her religion to leave her husband. If she left her abusive spouse, then she would be shunned by her family and friends. Still, it is easy to make assumptions while not walking a mile in the other person's shoes. I've been the abused wife and had no clue domestic abuse shelters even existed.

Back to walking or in the journalist's case, scooters. The general Indian population walks where they need to go, some use public transit when it is available, as well as scooters, bicycles, cars and the occasional ox wagon. Using a scooter doesn't mean you have a death wish. It does mean you can't afford a car. I noticed many of the women on them ride side saddle due to their long saris and yet they don't fall off which says a great deal about the driver's skill. Delhi is riddled with major speed bumps, so no one is going to be driving that fast anyhow.

Let's go back to the journalist's brief sweeping statement that those in India have a death wish because they use scooters without helmets. This is somehow connected with their belief in reincarnation. The actual law is the driver must wear a helmet and I noticed all did. In the United States, several states have no requirement for motorcyclists to wear helmets. Now, this makes you wonder who has a death wish because you can get up some speed on some American highways. In my own state, it is rare to see a motorcyclist with a helmet.

A quick search for stats revealed that in 2016 almost 26 percent of those surveyed in the United States did believe in reincarnation. This makes me think not only did the writer not walk a mile in scooter-riding Delhi inhabitant's shoes, but she also didn't take a wide view of facts to get a few laughs from her American readers.

There is also the inference that scooter riders don't care about their children. That's harsh. I noticed when traveling through India, there were no parents screaming at their children, which is standard at any shopping venues in the United States. In India, many new parents are often trying to get their baby enrolled in the better schools as soon as the child is born because there is a waiting list. Personally, I'm amazed how much income a parent will pay for their child's education. Family is all, which is demonstrated by the willingness of people to travel hundreds, even thousands of miles, for a wedding or family event. It must be a favorite relative before I'm boarding a plane for a wedding or driving across multiple states for an event.

In Michel Newton's book, *Journey of the Souls*, he points out that people we may view as failures by the society's standards are often the more enlightened souls. This could mean the homeless guy people make a wide berth around might know a bit more about true happiness than the Wall Street banker. I try to take a few minutes before spouting my opinion to the general public.

I may never understand runners or experience a runner's high; I'll leave it to them. No need to criticize them for their athletic pursuits because it is their business. It isn't better or worse than walking, but I prefer walking. When you get right down to it, it's a matter of preference. It's not facts. It's not what is right or wrong, it is just what an individual might like to do. Before we assume someone isn't doing something right, we need to take a step back and consider the big picture and the lack of options, too.

The smallest things we take for granted are often not available to other people around the world. This was brought home to me in the bathroom of the Indira Gandhi airport. A mother and daughter were in awe of a changing table fastened to the wall. They took turns opening and closing it as they excitedly chattered about it. To me, it was a standard convenience in public restrooms. For them, it may have been a game changer.

Assume nothing. Observe. Ask questions. Remember to think of the big picture, too. My Indian hosts may have found it odd that not only did I keep a dog in my house, but I had pictures of it on my phone, too. They were much too polite to mention this, though.

We would all do well to show the same restraint with meeting those with different preferences and cultural outlooks. It could help if we tried walking a mile in their shoes, too.

Measuring Success

ANYONE WHO WATCHES EVEN A day of television complete with commercials gets a good dose of what success is in the Western World. Success equals a sporty new car, a palatial house with a swimming pool, jetting off on an exotic vacation, an enviable wardrobe and figure, youth, and don't forget the attention of a sexy partner. Copywriters who write this stuff are told there are only two motivating factors to sell anything, fear and greed. Fear could include fear of missing out, too.

Other people measure success by time. Numerous people have bragged they'll be a millionaire by thirty or retire early at fifty. Others have. Money and shortchanging the usual work like a dog until you're sixty-five before you retire routine equals success. Back in the day, I dated a guy who had done this. Was he a success? By some people's standards, he was. In truth, he was a very lonely, miserable man. His relentless drive to accomplish this before he was fifty alienated his family and eventually his business partner, too. Ironically, because he was always 24/7 about work, he never developed any side interests or hobbies to keep him busy when he retired early. I stopped dating him because he had no compassion for anyone. He viewed most folks as stepping stones. His early retirement had him sitting alone in his big house watching television and drinking.

Do you have to live long to be a success? I've had friends who have died young usually by misadventure or accident. Up to the time they died, they lived happy, contented lives. Many people would say what a waste. No one is guaranteed seventy years or more. I consider my friends who died early as successes. Most of them may have liked a few more years. A familiar quote is, "it isn't how long you live, but the life within those years that matter." Time or long life isn't necessarily the answer.

Usually money is part of the equation of being successful, but usually those who aren't millionaires can rack up points by doing things faster than everyone else. Examples include graduating early, being a junior partner at a remarkably young age, or publishing a best seller at the age of twenty. These early milestones often do cause envy among older colleagues and friends, and cause conflict at work. At the age of twenty, I was promoted over women twice my age at a job that was only meant to pay my way through college.

Women who had worked there for twenty years or more were in the position of taking orders from a kid. My boss promoted me because she saw potential in me. In other words, she saw what I could be, not what I was. This was a real slap in the face to my fifty-something colleagues who had made their positions their career and not a filler position. Did I feel successful? Nope. I did feel very uncomfortable as angry stares bore into my back. I eventually asked my boss for my old position back citing I didn't have time to devote to the new one.

Relationships can define success, too. On a recent tour of an ancient tomb, the guide explained to us that various markings on a woman's grave showed if she died married or single. There were even elaborate curlicues to show if she married nobility or an average Joe. Even in death, the female couldn't escape being judged by marital status. Women used to be raised to marry well as their single purpose in life. Marrying well doesn't necessarily mean being part of a loving union, but it is more of the ability to move in the upper social circles and have so much plastic surgery you won't be recognizable to your old friends.

Then there are the years married success mark. It could be the silver or golden anniversary mark. Children usually put on a big celebration to mark this milestone. However, many who reach this age together are at the point where they basically nitpick each other and show no joy at being together. Debbie Ford, in her book entitled *Spiritual Divorce*, points out if a couple decides to go separate ways, it doesn't mean the relationship was a failure because you didn't get to celebrate any milestone anniversaries. Instead it means it was a relationship meant to last seven years or seven months depending on how long you were together. Relationship success isn't an endurance contest.

On the other hand, it is okay to be happy on your own. No television ads would spotlight someone contentedly walking the beach alone, but it happens. After my divorce, I was thrilled to be alone and think my own thoughts, and just eat food I liked. To some people, I was probably a sad, pitiful creature since I didn't measure up to the popular image of success.

As an aging person, I notice my friends who are of similar age have grown depressed about the changes they've witnessed in their bodies and mind. There seems to be no place for arthritic knees or saggy jowls on the success podium. We do not value the elderly for their wisdom in the Western Society. A talented, experienced employee will be replaced with a younger, cheaper version. In Asian countries, I noticed the elderly are treated with respect and reverence. Most of these elderly folks do seem happier because they have reached a time that is equated with success in their culture.

Good looks, at least for women, has always been valued, which goes back to marrying well. What is defined as attractive keeps changing, too. Back in Elizabethan times, it was a high hairline, and women used to shave their heads to achieve the big forehead. Women were also swallowing arsenic to achieve translucent skin and mysteriously dying early. Today women battle eating disorders, use hair extensions, and false eyelashes to acquire the Photoshopped image of beauty that even models can never reach. When we aren't enough, we reach out to others to define our achievements.

Many parents attempt to live through their children to obtain the elusive success label. There is the old trope of the Jewish mother who starts every sentence with *my son, the doctor.* Many parents consider themselves a success if their child has a high-paying career. On the other hand, if their child decides to be an artist, actress, or yoga instructor, then they failed—unless they become very famous in their field. Leonard Nimoy's parents refused to pay for their son's college when he chose acting. Their goal was to persuade their son to choose an acceptable career. He didn't. He worked his way through school and became renowned as Mr. Spock in the *Star Trek* series.

When my children were small, I was asked what did I want them to be when they grew up. This question implied that I had some type of choice over their careers and future lives, which I didn't. My reply was I wanted them to be happy.

Happiness is essentially a very personal creation. It does take reflection to decide what that is for each person. Sometimes, all it takes is a change of perspective, too. I resigned a job where I felt my efforts were unappreciated. Several jobs later, I realized that was probably my dream job, but I left it because I had unrealistic expectations.

If we allow commercials to define what success is, then we are bound to be disappointed. The whole point behind advertising is to sell stuff. People chasing the commercial idea have about a week of happiness or less with their new purchase. Soon they are longing for the next best thing. University of Colorado researcher, Leaf Van Boven, found people are happier with experiences as opposed to things. Experiences can be relived in memory, shared, discussed, and of course, there are photos, too. In this case, travel can make you happy. Only if you do it right though.

On a recent flight home, a nearby traveler complained about the temperature of the plane as if the attendant could correct it. She refused all food choices, criticizing them and saying she couldn't eat them and wanted something different. The food on the plane was quite good, as was the service, but this traveler was determined to be unhappy. Travel, like most of life, requires a certain amount of compromise, too.

Travel won't necessarily fulfil the Western Society idea of success unless you travel to the heavily advertised venues such as Disney World, Las Vegas, or a luxurious cruise. Success must be defined as to what you see success as. Keep in mind, your definition will always be changing. After spending three weeks in a noisy city, we were pleased to come home to our quiet, tree-filled neighborhood. My definition changes with exposure to other places.

The best example of achieving the dream is a woman I worked with long ago. By beauty standards, she was not a success with her ordinary features and her weight tipping the scales to the heavy side. Her enthusiasm for life and delight in every little thing made her a joy to work with.

She and her husband eked out a living barely making an above minimum wage and lived in a sub-standard apartment. They would not be most people's standard of success. Even though my co-worker was very easy to get along with, other employees were openly envious of her. They resented her good relationship with her husband and her consistent cheerful attitude. In some ways, she must have been a success since she inspired envy in others.

What is your perfect world? Your dream existence? Mine is filled with trees, starry skies, and a half dozen rescue dogs, along with leisure time spent with my husband. It would include time to write, read, and dream. But wait a minute, I already have that, except for a few more dogs and I'm working on that.

Sources

"10 Real Risks of Multitasking, to Mind and Body." *Psychology Today*, Sussex Publishers, www.psychologytoday.com/us/blog/the-squeaky-wheel/201606/10-real-risks-multitasking-mind-and-body.

"A Day Without a Mexican." *Wikipedia*, Wikimedia Foundation, 6 Feb. 2019, en.wikipedia.org/wiki/A_Day_Without_a_Mexican.

"Age Distribution – Religion in America: U.S. Religious Data, Demographics, and Statistics." *Pew Research Center's Religion & Public Life Project*, 11 May 2015, www.pewforum.org/religious-landscape-study/age-distribution.

Boehrer, Katherine. "Which of Your Favorite Foods Are Hiding A Massive Water Footprint?" *HuffPost*, HuffPost, 31 Dec. 2018, www.huffpost.com/entry/food-water-footprint_n_5952862.

Britannica, The Editors of Encyclopedia. "Gene Roddenberry." *Encyclopedia Britannica*, Encyclopedia Britannica, Inc., 14 June 2019, www.britannica.com/biography/Gene-Roddenberry.

Bruneau, Megan, and M. A. "5 Things Everyone Should Know About Acceptance." *Mindbodygreen*, Mindbodygreen, 4 July 2015, www.mindbodygreen.com/0-13730/5-things-everyone-should-know-about-acceptance.html.

"DEFENDING MEAT: VEGETARIAN MYTH #3 – BEEF IS UNACCEPTABLY WATER-INTENSIVE." *EPIC Provisions*, epicprovisions.com/blogs/land-livestock/defending-meat-vegetarian-myth-3-beef-is-unacceptably-water-intensive.

Diàna Markosian, Richard Grant. "Do Trees Talk to Each Other?" *Smithsonian.com*, Smithsonian Institution, 1 Mar. 2018, www.smithsonianmag.com/science-nature/the-whispering-trees-180968084.

Eadie, Betty J., and Curtis Taylor. Embraced by the Light. *Bantam Books*, 2002.

"Experiences Make People Happier Than Material Goods, Says University of Colorado Prof." *ScienceDaily*, ScienceDaily, 28 Dec. 2004, www.sciencedaily.com/releases/2004/12/041219182811.htm.

"Federal Bureau of Prisons." *BOP Statistics: Inmate Race*, www.bop.gov/about/statistics/statistics_inmate_race.jsp.

Gladwell, Malcolm. *Blink: The Power of Thinking without Thinking*. Back Bay Books, 2013.

Gottlieb, Lori. Marry Him: The Case for Settling for Mr. Good Enough. *Text Publishing Company*, 2011.

Grief.com, grief.com/the-five-stages-of-grief.

"*Happy.*" Belic, Roko, director. 2013.

Hesse, Hermann, and Stanley Appelbaum. *Siddhartha*. Dover Publications, 1999.

Li, Qing. "*The Benefits of 'Forest Bathing'*." *Time*, Time, 1 May 2018,
time.com/5259602/japanese-forest-bathing.

Mailonline, Harry Pettit For. "Plants Have Feelings Too! Shrub
Leaves Warn Their Neighbours of Danger through a Nervous
System." *Daily Mail Online*, Associated Newspapers, 14 Sept.
2018, www.dailymail.co.uk/sciencetech/article-6168395/Plants-
feelings-Shrub-leaves-warn-neighbours-danger-nervous-
system.html.

Matheson, Richard. *The Enemy Within*, NBC, 1966.

Moore, Dinty W. The Accidental Buddhist: Mindfulness,
Enlightenment, and Sitting Still, American Style. *Broadway
Books*, 2001.

Noire, Rayna. Communicating with Your Animal Messengers.
Sleeping Dragon Press, 2017

"Poultry Farming." *Wikipedia*, Wikimedia Foundation, 5 July 2019,
en.wikipedia.org/wiki/Poultry_farming.

Remarque, Erich Maria, and A. W. Wheen. All Quiet on the
Western Front. *Little, Brown*, 1996.

Silverstein, Shel. The Giving Tree. *HarperCollins*, 1999.

Smith, Jeffrey. "10 Reasons to Avoid GMOs." *Institute for
Responsible Technology*, 16 Jan. 2017,
responsibletechnology.org/10-reasons-to-avoid-gmos.

"Social Media Increases Depression and Loneliness." *Healthline*,
Healthline Media, www.healthline.com/health-news/social-
media-use-increases-depression-and-loneliness.

"Star Trek." *Wikipedia*, Wikimedia Foundation, 1 July 2019, en.wikipedia.org/wiki/Star_Trek.

"The Beauty Myth – Naomi Wolf – E-Book." *HarperCollins Publishers: World-Leading Book Publisher*, www.harpercollins.com/9780061969942/the-beauty-myth.

Tolle, Eckhart. The Power of Now: A Guide to Spiritual Enlightenment. *Namaste Publishing*, 2004.

"Women and the Negativity Receptor." *Oprah.com*, www.oprah.com/omagazine/why-women-have-low-self-esteem-how-to-feel-more-confident/all.

www.ingramcontent.com/pod-product-compliance
Lightning Source LLC
LaVergne TN
LVHW041219080426
835508LV00011B/1000